Thomas Dixon

The Failure of Protestantism in New York and its Causes

Thomas Dixon

The Failure of Protestantism in New York and its Causes

ISBN/EAN: 9783337416263

Printed in Europe, USA, Canada, Australia, Japan

Cover: Foto ©Lupo / pixelio.de

More available books at **www.hansebooks.com**

OF

PROTESTANTISM

IN NEW YORK

AND ITS CAUSES.

BY

THOMAS DIXON, Jr.,

Pastor of the People's Church, Academy of Music, New York.

SECOND EDITION.

New York:

THE STRAUSS & REHN PUBLISHING CO.,

1896.

Dedicated

TO

GEO. D. HERRON,

A Modern Prophet of the Kingdom of God,
Professor of Applied Christianity
in Iowa College.

AUTHOR'S INTRODUCTORY NOTE.

This little book says and proves that Protestantism is a failure in New York. Three answers have already been hurled at my head by the Theological Grannies in this neighborhood. "You are an infidel!" "You are a sensationalist!" "You are a failure yourself!" Quite true, dear grannies, from your point of view. But the answers are irrelevant.

I might be an infidel with full grown horn, hoof and tail, and still Protestantism be a failure in New York, or I might be so supremely orthodox as to believe that Pope Leo XIII. is the scarlet woman of the Apocalypse, and that every man who differs with me in this view is a liar, a thief, a hypocrite, a brute or a Jesuit—and still Protestantism might be a failure in New York.

Then, suppose I am a sensationalist. What of it? Truth is stranger than fiction, and nature more miraculous than miracle. The most sensational discoveries of this century have all been simple facts. A statement may be sensational, and its author a prophet or a clown, a philosopher or a fool, and yet it may be a fact.

Again, it may be true that I am a failure—all the greater pity since I am a Protestant minister! This is not an answer. It is a confirmation. It is a confession. This is simply piling on the agony!

While I dislike the business of these denominational worthies, which is simply the perpetuation of ignorance by the use of the printing press, I assure them of my kindliest personal feelings, and still hope for the best.

T. D., Jr.

New York, February 5, 1896.

PREFACE TO SECOND EDITION.

It has been a gratifying surprise to me that this little book goes into its second edition within nine months, in spite of the real agonies of our political crisis. It has been the policy of the Church press in and around New York to carefully ignore it, and thus deny a hearing. The plan has not worked. Beloved, you have or will frankly and promptly meet the issues raised. It must be done sooner or later. The sooner the better. To my surprise the Roman Catholic press has uniformly given fair and intelligent revises of the book in spite of its explicit criticisms of the Roman policy and hopes.

T. D., Jr.

New York, Dec. 1, 1896.

Only a Few of the Many Press Reviews of First Edition.

From the New York "World."

"The Failure of Protestantism in NEW YORK and its causes" is full of pepper and spice; that will not delight the orthodox, but its facts deserve the attention of thoughtful men, however much they may disagree with the remedies proposed by the writer.

From the "Review of Reviews."

Mr. Dixon is known for the stirring and intense quality of his preaching upon the practical questions of the day, and he has in this little volume heaped up a most terrible indictment of the Protestant churches in the city of New York for their failure to do their proper work and to hold their own in their community. It is by recognizing facts rather than ignoring them that true progress is accomplished, and it will be better for the churches if they take Mr. Dixon's statistics and arguments to heart with a view of profiting by them.

President Geo. A. Gates, in the "Kingdom."

It is a terrific arraignment of the Protestant churches of New York city for the way they have run away, geographically and practically, from the awful physical and moral and spiritual needs of the city.

From the "New Church Messenger."

This is not a Roman Catholic book, as its name would at first suggest, but is a very live little volume written by a Protestant clergyman, and arraigns all denominations of the Church in this City, including the Catholic. Mr. Dixon's style is vigorous and many of his utterances might make good aphorisms. "Institutions that were of use in the past will have no place in the history of the future. They may have belonged to the history of the infancy of the race, but have no part in the story of the race's manhood." "The cry Back to the old paths, is the feeble rallying call of a reminiscent senility." "The Church must either lead or be led in this world movement of the race. We are now in the first years of the reign of the common people." "Uniformity gained by force does not mean unity. The belief that it does is the one tragic superstition of our history." But "The Failure of Protestantism" which it would be more appropriate to name "The Failure of Churchism" is not all a criticism. It believes in the Christian religion, and describes the "religion of the future" which must be "progressive," "simple," "in harmony with reason," "luminous," with a "saving" and a "social" power, and "characterized by common sense."

On the whole we greet "The Failure of Protestantism" with great pleasure. It is in, perhaps, rather a modest external form, but it is vigorous, purposeful, hopeful through its severest criticisms, and abounding in suggestive and helpful conceptions. If our readers should enjoy the perusal of this little volume half as much as we, it would well repay being purchased and read.

From the Jamaica (West Indies) "Post."

It is clever; it is manly and outspoken; and at times it is even eloquent and inspiriting.

Mr. Dixon is a young man of strong convictions; and he has the courage of his convictions. The same fearless spirit which he displays at the Academy of Music, he exhibits in every page of this book. It matters not to him whether his words are palateable to his friends and his brethren in the ministry, or whether they are calculated to drive them all mad with anger and chagrin. Sufficient for him that they are true—or, rather, that he thinks they are true. At all costs the truth must be told. That is his creed, as it is also his practice. And very cleverly and epigrammatically does he somtimes state his facts.

As an ardent Protestant, however, Mr. Dixon reserves his choicest vials of wrath for the Protestant denominations. He exposes and denounces mercilessly the tendency of all Protestant congregations to "move up-town"—to leave the squalid, crowded parts of the city, and to build churches only in "aristocratic" quarters. With an indignation worthy of one of the prophets of old he also holds up to scorn the custom that exists in so many congregations of appointing as office-bearers only such men as have long bank-accounts and occupy a good social position.

Altogether, Mr. Dixon has produced a notable book; and it would be a good thing if every minister of religion (Protestant and Catholic) throughout the English-speaking world could obtain a copy of it and read it. Towards the close of the volume he puts in a powerful plea for a simpler creed—for less theology and more religion—for an adaptation, in short, of the Church's message and methods to the wants of the age.

CONTENTS.

1. THE FACT OF THE FAILURE.
2. DISMANTLED CHURCHES AND DESERTED THOUSANDS.
3. PROTESTANTISM BECOMING A BOURGEOIS ARISTOCRACY.
4. THE CHURCH OF CHRIST A DEMOCRACY.
5. SECTARIANISM.
6. DEAD THEOLOGIES.
7. THE SUCCESS OF THE SALVATION ARMY.
8. THE APPARENT SUCCESS OF THE EPISCOPAL CHURCH.
9. THE STRENGTH OF ROMAN CATHOLICISM.
10. THE DECAY OF ROMANISM.
11. GOODY-GOODISM AND THE SCOURGE OF CHRIST.
12. THE RELIGION OF THE FUTURE.

APPENDIX.

"WHAT ARE THE CHURCHES GOING TO DO ABOUT IT?"

THE FAILURE OF PROTESTANTISM
In New York and its Causes.

CHAPTER I.

The Fact of the Failure.

As a Protestant, I have said that Protestantism in New York is a failure. For this assertion, I have been bitterly assailed. The man who shows intellectual hospitality is always accursed by a class of self-constituted guardians of the faith—that faith, in particular, on which their own personal interests turn. They have damned me as a renegade and traitor for making this aggravating declaration.

And yet facts are facts. Let us examine them. The assertion that I have made is the utterance of a sorrowful heart. It is based on six years of the hardest work and toughest experience of my life; experiences that have written themselves in grey lines in a young and over-hopeful head.

Why cannot a Protestant, in love, speak the truth about that which most deeply concerns him, and try to tell the truth, the whole truth and nothing but the truth about it? Has a preacher any more right to juggle with facts than any other man? Is lying wrong only in the sinner? Has the preacher the right to lie about his business, to put on a bold face and declare that he is enjoying a boom, when, as a matter of fact, he is a bankrupt and his property should be in the sheriff's hands? If we would heed the squeak of the sectarian hand-organ, yes; if the preacher possesses common honesty, no. Before any evil can be remedied we must face the facts—all the facts. We must squarely face them without whine or apology. Ours is a century of light, knowledge, investigation, analysis, facts. Woe to that creed or cult that dares to flinch beneath the searchlight of the dawning century. It is dead already.

THE SECTARIAN TEMPERAMENT.

There is a certain kind of mind that refuses to face facts which are disagreeable. This, pre-eminently, is the sectarian temperament. Dr. Momerie says that when the subject of evolution first began seriously to disturb the peace of the Church of England, a dear old maid of much churchly zeal sought her rector in a great state of mind over the matter. She begged the doctor to fully explan to her the utter absurdity of such a doctrine. The rector's explanations, however, were anything but reassuring. He told her that he must be perfectly frank with her and say that the preponderance of scientific evidence seemed now to indicate that God did use some such method in creating the world. She was horrified. She studied a moment and then tearfully exclaimed: "Oh, doctor, it is too terrible to think of our illustrious ancestors and those chattering monkeys—but, if you really think it is so, for heaven's sake do let's hush it up!"

That policy may work for a while. But the facts will be known at last. And then?

THE POSITION AND POWER OF NEW YORK.

What are the facts as to the condition and progress of Protestantism in New York to-day? New York's position and power are such as to afford a supreme test of modern Protestant methods. She is the centre of the commerce, society, art, literature, politics and religion of the Western World, and her port, in which float the flags of every nation, is the open gateway of two worlds. The feet of three million human beings press her pavements daily in the conflict of modern life. Here is the scorching furnace in which are being tried by fire the faiths, the hopes, the dreams, the memories, of that humanity that shall rule the earth in the twentieth century. The wealth, the power, the position of such a city are undisputed. New York City, in mere volume of population, is the equal of three of our great states. There is a single family on Fifth Avenue, whose wealth is greater than the entire valuation of the State of North Carolina with its 1,600,000 inhabitants and 48,580 square miles of land. Such a city sums up, in its fevered life, the conflict of the race in embryo. As the centre of the activities of humanity, its history is of supreme importance. In the sweep of that resistless progress before us will our pet faiths, fad and manners survive ? In the roar of this modern Babylon is religion increasing its hold on man ? It is doubtful.

HOLDING OUR OWN.

Is Protestantism growing stronger here ? The question is absurd to any man who lives in New York.

Is Protestantism even holding its own ? Some contend that it is. Nothing could be more absurd. Progress or retrogression are the inexorable laws of life. Nothing that lives can merely hold its own. It must increase or decrease its powers of vitality. A man must either grow better or grow worse, wiser or more stupid, stronger or weaker. To stop is to die. New York City is one of the most godless, if not the most godless city in America. The growth of churches and the growth of population shows that the vitality of Protestantism has declined steadily during the last forty years.

The following table shows the apparent gain in church membership during the last decade in leading Protestant Churches.

	1885.	1887.	1891.	1892		
Methodist	12,588	12,981	13,280	14,140	Net increase	1552
Baptist	13,669	13,687	13,952	14,644	Net increase	975
Presbyterian	20,308	23,016	23,299	24,737	Net increase	4429
Lutheran	14,000	14,000	.....	13,375	Net decrease	625

14   *THE FACT OF THE FAILURE.*

How long will it take these churches to take the world at this rate? Are they holding their own?

The Baptists increased 975 during the seven years 1885 to 1892. The normal birth-rate of their membership 13,669, should have given an increase by birth of more than 3,500 during this period; their accessions from other Baptist churches more than balancing their death-rate. The Baptists, therefore, managed to hold about one-fourth of the children born into their homes. Is this "holding our own"?

The Methodists increased 1,552 during these seven years. The birth-rate should give the Methodists in this time about 3,521. So our Methodist friends, with their matchless zeal, managed to hold nearly one-half the children born in their homes. Is this "holding our own"?

The Presbyterians increased 4,429 during these seven years. Their normal birth-rate should have given them an increase of 5,684. So our Presbyterian friends, with their enormous wealth and prestige, peculiar to New York City, massed in their 81 churches, managed to hold about two-thirds of the children born in their homes. Is this "holding our own"?

The Lutherans, with 14,000 members in 1885, show an actual decrease in roll of 625. Their birth-rate should have given them 3,920 increase. They have not only failed to hold their own children but have lost 625 of the older ones. Surely this is holding our own with a vengeance.

THE LIVING AND THE DEAD ENROLLED.

But these figures do not tell all the pitiable story. Every one knows who knows anything about the history of New York churches that the rolls are not kept to-day as they were twenty or thirty years ago. Then church enrollment meant a pretty accurate summary of the members on the field; now some of our churches keep even the dead on their rolls, on the ground that their establishment extends over this world and the next! One of these mushroom records collapsed the other day by a fire, and out of a roll of over 4,000 there could not be found 200 members! This is undoubtedly an extreme case, but it is to the point. There are actually fewer Baptists in New York to-day than there were twenty years ago; there are fewer Methodists than there were twenty years ago.

CHURCHES AND POPULATION.

While we have been thus holding our own with such remarkable vigor, what has the population of New York City been doing? The statistics of the churches and the population tell the sad story. These records of churches and population mean all churches—Catholic and Protestant.

1840—170 churches—312,852 population—1 to 1,840.
1892—569 churches—1,801,739 population—1 to 3,166.

Apparently we had 1 church to 1,840 people in the year 1840. In 1892 we had held our own to the extent of figuring out on paper 1 church to 3,166 people! I say figuring out on paper advisedly, for this record of churches is even more misleading than the record of members. In 1840 it was the policy of the Baptist churches, for example, to aim at the establishment only of vigorous self-supporting bodies, and, as a rule, the record of a church meant something. Now what are the facts? The Baptists report 51 churches in New York in 1894. I am personally acquainted with the history and present condition of every one of these so-called churches. To my certain knowledge 24 of these 51 recorded "Churches" merely represent aspiration, not attainment. They are utterly insignificant in membership, position, property or influence in the community. Some of them are, in fact, mission stations for reaching our foreign population, and many of them are not able to pay for heating and lighting, and sweeping out their places of worship. This incapacity has been long chronic in many cases. If the record of Protestant Churches were made on the principles that entered into the definition of a "church" in 1840, the statistics of 1892 would show we actually

THE FACT OF THE FAILURE.

have in New York to-day 1 church to about 6,000 inhabitants, as contrasted with 1 to 1840, forty-five years ago. Nor does all this tell the story of the actual condition of the people and the churches in New York. Almost all our large and vigorous churches are jammed in the rich and sparsely settled districts of the city, where churches of any sort are least needed, while the dark teeming millions in the crowded districts are untouched by the remotest influence from church life. Broome Street Tabernacle is a mission station of the New York City Mission and Tract Society and is supported by that Society. It is the only Protestant Church in the midst of a population of over 60,000. There are districts in New York of 50,000 inhabitants in which there is not found a single church of any sort. It is a conservative estimate that places the number of heathen in New York at 500,000.

WHERE ARE THE MEN?

The Federal Census of 1890 gives 135,000 Protestant communicants in New York. Probably twenty-five per cent. or about 33,000 of them are men. Out of a male population of 900,000, a little over three per cent. are Protestants. A vote that amounts to only three per cent. of a total poll is generally called scattering, and need not be considered! Besides, these people entered as Protestants in the Census, do not all of them go to church. I have counted the people present at a regular afternoon preaching service on a beautiful day in the largest Presbyterian church in the city, with a roll of 2,499 members and pews for 1,600 people—and there were just 425 people present! Probably, at the morning service, there were 850 present, but I greatly doubt it. In a prosperous, self-supporting Protestant church in New York, the congregation will generally average only forty per cent. of the church roll at the best service when the pastor is in his pulpit. There are, therefore, never more than 16,000 men to be found in the 451 Protestant churches in New York on the fairest day and under the very best conditions. The rest of the people are women and children. Where are the 900,000 men of New York on Sunday? They may be in the parks, they may be at Coney Island, they may lounge in the clubs or go a-fishing; but, wherever they are, they are rarely found crowding Protestant churches. There are 500 clubs and over 1,000 lodges in New York, and not a woman in them! Masonry alone counts 20,000 stalwart men in New York City.

THE MILLIONS INVESTED.

Let us look at it from another point of view—that of the invested capital and results. Methodism, undoubtedly, forms the most aggressive wing of Protestantism to-day in the New World. Last year the New York Conference West (including several strong suburban churches) reported 17,309 members in 86 churches. They gave to their work $550,000, and on an invested capital of $4,100,000 they gained net 241 members! Their birth-rate should have given them 692 new members, could they only succeed in holding their children. Think of it! An army of 17,309 soldiers massed in 86 divisions, spend $550,000 in a working capital on $4,100,000 investment and manage to save to their faith one-third of their own children. And they are supposed to be in a field campaign conquering the world. If an ordinary business man at the end of the year were confronted with such results in the conduct of his trade—he would do one of two things—speedily change his methods, or call in the sheriff and sell out the whole thing as junk! The Baptists in the Southern New York Association, including several powerful suburban churches, reported in 1894, 18,604 members. During the four years from 1891 to 1894 they gave on an average $500,000 annually, an aggregate of $2,000,000 in these four years. They have 68 churches and their property in worth $4,000,000. From '91 to '94 they spent $2,000,000 in a working capital on $4,000,000 invested and managed to gain 216 members annually. Their birth rate was 744 annually. How long will it take the Baptists at this rate to conquer the world?

The Presbyterians in New York give annually at least $1,000,000. Their property is worth over $8,000,000 and they average a gain of 632 annually. Is this all? No! American Presbyterianism with its enormous wealth and established power has done one more thing for the cause of Christianity in New York— expelled from the pulpit Prof. Charles A. Briggs, the foremost scholar of the Church of Christ in the New World. Truly this is progress.

DESERTS OF EMPTY PEWS.

What is the character of the average attendance on Protestant church services in New York? The plain fact is Protestantism has little hold on the manhood of New York. The men have deserted the churches and built clubs and secret societies in their stead. The attendance on the average smaller churches that cannot command preachers of great personal powers is simply beneath contempt. I shall never forget my first experience in a great city church. I was fresh from the far-off South, full of fire and zeal. I knew the church building had a capicity of 1,500 and that they had 1,600 members. My own little village church barely held 400. I dreamed of a sea of eager living faces. I trusted to the inspiration of the hour to give me my best thought. The eventful morning of my life came. Shall I ever forget it? I sat down shivering in the pulpit, the blood in my veins fairly frozen at the sight before me—a desert of empty benches with just 80 human beings scattered among them. I stumbled through the service somehow. I tried to preach but I could not. The sight of that silent and solemn mausoleum, and those prim elderly women and a few fidgety old men looking up at me from their lonely perches took all the soul out of me. I made the most stupid failure of my life. It makes me shiver to think of that December morning now. This is no exceptional case. It has long been the rule in the average Protestant church in lower New York. Dr. Shauffler, the veteran mission worker of the city made, from the platform of Chickering Hall some time ago, the following statement: "I made the rounds some time ago on a beautiful Sunday morning in some of these churches, and some of them fairly large—and this was the count: in four churches there was one with 126 people, another 35, another 25, and another 110. If anybody tells you that he estimates that in his church there are 500 in the congregation you can cut him down 50 per cent. and you will be about right. The next Sunday was a beautiful Sunday and I went forth once more to count the people, and I found them. In 4 churches—there were 55 in one, 45, 28, and in another 26, and a bright Sunday morning it was too."

A man said to another, in New York, one day: "How do you account for the small attendance on the Protestant churches?"

"I can't account for it at all," replied his friend. "I went to one of them the other night myself, and for the life of me I couldn't make out what under heaven brought as many people there as I saw. It's too much for me, I can't understand it."

SACRED REFRIGERATORS.

Not only is the average service of the average Protestant church, as at present conducted in New York, inexpressibly dull, but the religious fibre of the stronger ones is unquestionably tough. It is the almost universal experience of young people who come into New York from the country that they are chilled to the marrow of their bones by their first contact with our church life. They rarely recover their spiritual equilibrium after this first disillusion.

They desert the churches of their childhood, and join the great church outside of the Church that grows faster with each succeeding generation. The plain truth is, fashion and pride and wealth, and social caste, for their own sake, dominate our strongest churches. The best attended of these great churches are crowded simply by the social attraction of the wealthy families who rule them. To keep out the herd of vulgar, social aspirants who wish to scrape acquaintance by jostling the children of the rich, some of these churches have separate Sunday-schools for the rich and the poor. Really we cannot blame them in view of the evident motive of this mob. And yet, is this Christianity? A pastor was recently driven out of a fashionable church for two reasons. First, they said he was not an orator. Second, they said he gave too much time to the poor! "Has the Messiah come, or shall we look for another?" What answer could these people give to the Disciples of John, if they should come to-day seeking the sign of their discipleship of Jesus?

THE PROPHETS DEAD.

New York is the largest graveyard of Protestant preachers in America. Toward the dazzling light of its metropolitan life they flock from the smaller cities. Against its adamantine surface they dash their brains out like bewildered birds around a lighthouse. New York kills more preachers than any city in America. They start off well and work well for a few months, perhaps a year or so, and then they quietly die. They may still fill their pulpits and deceive the census taker and be rated among the living. But God knows they are dead, and man has ceased to care one way or the other. A prophetic, authoritative ministry has all but ceased to exist in New York.

THE SMUG NEW YORKER.

The pew dominates the pulpit. Such is the age of the Scribe and Pharisee. A prophet cannot grow under such a blight. The noblest prophetic instincts of the Protestant ministry have been strangled. They wear collars. They choke. When you pass the door you do not hear the clear ring of a prophet's voice. You merely hear a wheeze.

Rural enthusiasms are soon crushed beneath the cold sarcasm of self-satisfied New Yorkism in the pews. Of all the forces I have ever encountered, this is the most stupefying. I know what the ignorance of the South is—it is my own fair, native land. I have lived in Boston, and know what the sullen traditionalism of New England means, with its bulldog tenacity. I have travelled West, and measured the boundless cheek of the typical Westerner, but for downright stupidity, for smug self-satisfaction, for hopeless incapacity in the world of morals and spirituality, I have encountered nothing on this earth that compares to the average half-well-to-do New Yorker. He has little brains, no culture—scarcely the rudiments of common sense—but being a New Yorker, he assumes everything! Of this big world outside the Bowery, Fifth Avenue, Coney Island and Central Park, he knows nothing, for he neither reads nor travels; and yet, without a moment's hesitation he sits in instant judgment upon the world movements of human thought and society. These are the men who are ruling the Protestant churches in New York—the big little men who hold the offices and dictate its methods and politics.

A few years ago a country Congressman in Washington was holding a most dignified conversation with one of his constituents. While talking, a careworn elderly looking man approached and asked the Congressman for a few moments of his valuable time. With evident annoyance he stepped aside. Upon returning he said with lofty scorn to his constituent: "What do you suppose that old fool is worrying the life out of me about? He wants me to use my influence to induce Congress to stretch a wire from Washington to Baltimore so that one fool over there can talk forty miles to a fool here!" And with infinite scorn this great man gazed after the retreating figure of Morse, the inventor of the telegraph. Such is the chronic attitude of the New York Protestant pew toward the prophet who dares to speak a real message. And so a dead past rules us in the living present.

SICK MEN AND SICK SOULS.

When George Washington was stricken with pneumonia, his secretary, Tobias Lear, says that the overseer was summoned, who took a half pint of blood from him. Mixtures of molasses, vinegar and butter were given, but to no effect. Gargles of sage-tea and bandages of flannel about his throat proved equally useless.

A physician arrived, bled him again, and ordered the same gargle, which "produced great distress and suffocation."

Another physician arrived and bled him again, administering drugs which also seemed still more to weaken the patient. Finding that the general was rapidly sinking, and feeling that the country would hold them responsible for the care of his life, the alarmed physicians consulted anxiously, and, as a last resort, bled him once more. Washington, feeling himself to be dying, sent for his will, gave directions concerning his papers, military records and the disposal of his body, and then prepared himself for death with the calmness of a stoic. "The physicians were absorbed in grief."

The poorest tramp who falls in an almhouse to-day has better attention. He commands the results of the knowledge of centuries. But for the sick in soul to-day, we insist on the same methods used by our forefathers hundreds of years ago. And we wonder why we fail. And in our bewilderment we become apostles of the gospel of geography. When we fail, we move up-town. When the town moves further up, we move again. Our apologists say that the people have moved. And yet we look to the east, to the west, to the north and to the south, and as far as the eye can reach rolls the sea of human life.

When the coroner brings in the true verdict on these dead churches, it will be this: "Drowned in an ocean of humanity, hunting for men."

Protestantism counts less than 35,000 men in 1,800,000 population in New York. Add to this 100,000 women and you have the total results of a century of toil and struggle and sacrifice.

Our invested capital is over $160,000,000; our annual gifts of money aggregate over $4,000,000 and we cannot hold the children born in our homes. Is this success or failure?

CHAPTER II.

Dismantled Churches and Deserted Thousands.

The supreme test of any religion is not so much its number of adherents and temples as its power to save the people. Its claims of authority are a hollow mocking upon their very face if made amid squalor and hunger, rags and pauperism, crime and despair. Confronted by this supreme crisis in New York, Protestantism has taken to its heels and fled up-town. One by one every influential church in the once prosperous down-town communities has given up the struggle and become apostles of the gospel of geography. As the mob follow them they move again, until they find breathing space at last amid the vacant lots, scattered palaces and browsing goats of the upper West Side. One of the historic churches of the Protestant denomination that stood near the Academy of Music has been demolished and a business building erected in its stead. And another that stood opposite has just been sold and converted into a beer garden. One of the largest and strongest churches of the Presbyterian denomination on Fourteenth Street has sold their church edifice and moved up-town. An historic church of another denomination, with a pastor whose name has been historic for twenty years, is now on the market, and its trustees ask $1,000,000 for the lot. Where the vacant church on Fourteenth Street stands, to-day surges such a tide of humanity as never surged before it since the day its foundation stone was laid. People gone! They have not gone; they have come. They have come in such numbers and with such problems—such questions, that churches have taken fright and fled before this flood, this avalanche, that threatens to engulf weakness and humbug Christianity!

The life of the down-town masses of the city is the strategetic point in the battle of Christianity with the modern world.

Here is the supreme test of the genuineness of our discipleship of Christ:

It is the disposition and power to save the lost and weak and helpless. John sent from prison to Christ to know in his condition of helplessness whether He were the Christ or they should expect another. Poor disheartened prophet! Pioneer and forerunner he had been in the early days, crying, "Prepare the way," and now overwhelmed with difficulties, imprisoned and deserted, his life hanging on the whim of a harlot, he sent to Christ, if He were the Messiah, to give him some sign that he might know that his hope and preaching had not been in vain.

What was the answer of Jesus Christ? He did not say: "Go back to John and tell him of the miracles that accompanied my entrance into the world; that the star stood over the manger in Bethlehem, and men from far Eastern worlds saw the supernatural manifestation and moved across the deserts that they might stand over the cradle and see the coming Saviour; that the angels came down from God and said to the shepherds on the hill on the night of my birth, 'Peace on earth, good-will to men.'" He sent back this message to John: "Go, tell him that you have seen and heard: that the lame walk, the blind see, the lepers are cleansed, the dead are raised," that he may know the kingdom is come—climax of all, "that the Gospel is preached to the poor, to the outcast world; He will know then."

OUT OF THE THE DITCH.

I stand to-day before the Church of Jesus Christ in this community, and in every modern community, and say it must answer that supreme test. It is useless to prate about the inspiration of the Bible, or this or that doctrine, if, in the vital struggle, in the hand-to-hand conflict with sin and hell, there is failure and retreat and defeat. The supreme test of Christianity is found in its power to reach our civilization and save it; reach our life and bless it, lift it from the ditch and plant it on the heights. If Christianity cannot answer that supreme test, it has failed in

DISMANTLED CHURCHES, ETC.

the one hour of its supreme trial. I come to-day before the Church of Christ in New York and ask that solemn test. Does the true church of Christ exist in New York to-day? It is no use to say: "See our sculptured poems in marble and glittering spires. See our magnificent frescoes, our beautiful pews." The one test in the genuineness of the discipleship of Christ is: Have you reached; are you saving the lost and lapsed world? Have the poor the Gospel preached to them? Do the lame walk? Are the blind being made to see? If not, then you have failed; then you are failing to-day.

THICKEST OF THE FIGHT.

Here around you surge the needy millions who are to be saved if this world is saved, because here the hosts of hell are marshaled, here the lost are marshaled, and Jesus said the Son of Man came to seek and save not the righteous, but that which was lost.

Jesus said the kingdom of heaven was like unto that of the lost sheep; to the woman who sought diligently the one coin lost; like the feast spread and the seats were vacant, and He said to the manager of the feast, "Go out into the highways and hedges and compel them to come in. Bring in the poor and lame, and halt and blind, that the table shall be filled." The church that bundles up its bag and baggage and flees before this tide of humanity gives up the struggle, has turned its back on the commission of Jesus Christ and on the Saviour who stood beside that dark multitude and wept as He looked at them, scattered as sheep without a shepherd.

NEW YORK AND LONDON.

Around the doors of the down-town churches surge this class of people of which Jesus spoke in His test to John.

The poor are here—poor in body in this world's goods; the poor in mind, and, above all, the poor in soul—poor in life. New York City is the most crowded city of the civilized world. London has seven people to a house; New York sixteen. There is no crowded district of all the civilized world in which property is so packed and so intensified, with all its hideous aspects and in so wide an area as in this metropolitan city of the New World, with its new hope and new life. Here, around the doors of your down-town church, you find the thousands of laboring people who sweat out their lives. Needlewomen who sew into the coats you wear their hearts' blood, until you can feel the throb of aching nerve in every seam.

The poor are around this down-town church, crowded in dark and dingy tenements, tier piled on tier, until it seems as if the filthy foundations of the buildings would groan at the burden of woe they bear.

JACOB RIIS'S REPORT.

Here are the districts where Mr. Riis found twelve men and women in one room thirteen feet square. It is in these districts that they sleep at five cents a spot, on the floor, on a table or shelf—anywhere they can find a place. It is in this district that children swarm like so many vermin. Mr. Riis found in two buildings 136 children in two dark and dingy holes. Death stalks through these crowded alleys with his scythe always swinging. From a thousand doors in summer there flutter each week the white ribbons which tell of broken hearts and homes.

Here are found the blind. You can find them in this district staggering from those saloons whose doors swing on their gilded hinges every day in the year.

In no district of the city is the curse of the saloon, with its beautiful surroundings, its music and companionship, and all that degrades—in no district is its curse so terrible as in these districts to which God has called the down-town church to minister. Here are found the lame. The foreign world is crowded here, groping in its blind way after life, not able to read the signboards that might point to life, the easy victim of every darkened soul that seeks to destroy. In a single district of this city there are 111,000 people crowded, nearly every one of whom are foreigners, blind in finding the way of life.

A STERN TRIBUNAL.

Think you that with them will perish the evil they have wrought? No; in that district, with 111,000 crowded souls, there are 23,000 children. I think of the hosts that press the pavements of Cherry Hill, and of the few who are born to the world on the heights of fashion, and I look into the faces of those dirty urchins, stained with mud, and their hearts stained with crime, and it seems to me that I can hear the step of a coming army whose breathings are not for the life of the nation or of the Church.

I hear the coming tread of a generation of men who not only know not the name of Jesus Christ, but who do not even know the name of the government in which they were born; who do not know the flag under which they are supposed to march as citizens, who one day may stand before a staggering State and challenge it to make good its own life before the stern tribunal of the guillotine, the dagger, the torch and the dynamite bomb! Those children growing up in those districts without Christ or the knowledge of truth, or the influence of civilization, cannot be left alone with impunity. If you do not love them they will make you look after them to save your own life, bye and bye.

Lepers there are around the doors of this church. The outcasts of society, the fallen women congregated in these districts, whose touch is pollution, the criminals pouring forth in renewed streams, the evil influences of an evil life. The dead are here, men dead to hope, dead to life, to civilization, to honor, to all the influences that make life worth living for you and me.

BLACK-WHEELED GUNS.

Those marching hosts of thousands of children in those districts who do not know the name of Christ, will have a settlement with you and the State in the future.

In your midst to-day, there is a population of 50,000, whose only restraint from torch and knife and bomb, is the fact that in your armories there stand black-wheeled guns that can be drawn into the streets and sweep them with grape and canister. The only power to-day that stands to guard your life, is that power which is itself the abrogation of civilization and the inauguration of the Reign of Terror and Death.

Think you these people can be left to work out their own salvation? The time will come in the life of the men who tear up their churches and move them to the grand boulevards of the north, when a heavy hand may knock at their barred doors and ask of them the reason for their existence.

MOAN OF THE GREAT SEA.

Here lie the lapsed thousands with their awful needs. Here rolls that dark sea of human want and woe across which Jesus walked, and with voice of love cried, "Peace be still." And shall they who bear the name of Jesus, flee before that moan of misery that breaks to-day on the shores of our city? The church that deserts does it at the peril of its life.

If the gospel fails to reach and save these people, to whom shall they go? "Master, thou hast the word of eternal life; to whom can we go?" Their daily lot is a poverty that means hunger and cold, and nakedness and rags. It is this shadow that falls across the streets of the city as nowhere else on the earth to-day. There are poor people in the country, but they are millionaires in all that constitutes life as compared with the poor of the city.

It is a continuous amazement to me that people should leave the country and crowd into the city; the city which Carlyle graphically described, "The great foul city, rattling, crawling, smoking, stinking, a ghastly heap of fermented brickwork, pouring out poison at every pore." And yet they come in tens, in hundreds, in thousands, in tens of thousands every year, crowding the already crowded trades, crowding the already crowded dens in which human beings whelp and stable like beasts. They leave clear skies. They leave pure air. They leave kindly friends, sympathetic neighbors. They leave earth for hell, and still they come. Such poverty in the city means the loss of a home. There is no home life among the poor of the great city. The word home is stricken from the language of man. The poor live in a den. They exist in a tenement, and the tenement life, with its attendant horrors, is constantly on the increase in our great cities. In New York City it has swallowed up all the other life practically. The tenement has, like a huge monster, devoured the home.

It may be said that New York City lives in the tenements; in the second and third-class tenements. One million three hundred thousand people in this city exist in second and third-class tenements. This constitutes the people. The landlords are an insignificant faction. People who live in separate houses are not of the people; they are the exception. To every so-called house in the City of New York there is an average of sixteen dwellers. London averages seven. In what is known as the tenement house district there are no fewer than 276,000 families packed together. In this quarter it goes without saying that the death-rate reaches its most horrible height, and public morality touches a depth of degradation before which philanthropists stand aghast. Such poverty is the open door to theft because the wages are so low that the temptation to wrongdoing is well-nigh resistless. How hundreds and thousands of people in the cities, with their wages, can keep from stealing is a miracle. A man is certainly entitled to existence. He is entitled to enough clothes to keep him from freezing. He is entitled to a house to cover his head, and he has a right to work. But these things are denied hundreds and thousands of people to-day in the city. A woman was discovered the other day who had starved to death. Men commit crime daily that they may get the comforts of a penitentiary, the luxury of a stay on Blackwell's Island. The children born are doomed before their birth, and the generation that rises has less of hope than the generation that dies. Our statisticians tell us that 20,000 children work in the great city of New York; but those who know the facts tell us that in the great city of New York alone there are 100,000 little pinched forms that work for their daily bread and are glad to get work —work at the period when children must grow or die. Their little faces are pinched and shriveled and wrinkled until they are an army of little men and women. What wonderful creatures many of them are! They never complain—they take it as a matter of course.

There are 60,000 of these little waifs drifting on the black waters of this city's life, and every city has its proportion. Is it any wonder that we have tramps and idlers, and that the gang of toughs is soon developed, and that they graduate into the hardened criminal, desperado, highwayman and assassin?

PANTS SEVEN CENTS A PAIR.

Woman is the mother of civilization as well as the mother of man. Womanhood is the index to life. If it be degraded, life is degraded. If it is steeped in sullen despair, life will show its fruits. If it be hard, life will be hard. If the life of woman leads to hell, hell is nigh to humanity. Two hundred and fifty thousand women work at hard tasks outside of domestic service in this city. Three hundred and forty-three trades are open to women, the census-taker tells us. They are, as a matter of fact, simply subdivisions caused by the divisions of labor. Added to this is the additional horror of unpaid labor. There is not a single one of these lower trades in which women work in which they are actually paid a just return for their labor. Because they are women, they are made to do the work which men could not do better, for from one-third to one-half the remuneration men would receive.

Needlewomen make pants for 7 cents a pair, and use their own machines, find their own thread. They make shirts for 35 cents a dozen, and find their own thread and machines. They make gingham waists for boys at 2½ cents each, and it is impossible to make more than a dozen in 14 hours at a sewing-machine. And 14 hours at a sewing-machine, with a woman's hands and a woman's nerves, means that life is being ground out at a pace that makes the thing little short of murder. Cloakmakers can earn but 60 to 70 cents a day. We find 16 hours of toil, unrelieved by a single gleam of light or hope or cheer, and the net results of this concentrated despair and misery is $3.50 a week. And half of this is taken to pay for the den in which the work is done. Two families live in single rooms. Twelve people are found sometimes in a room 13 feet square.

Many of the women who work in this underworld of horror are dying to hope, and when woman, with her ceaseless passion of life, her undying love, with her quenchless heroism, ceases to hope, it is time for your preacher, your politician, your philosopher, to hasten to find the cause.

NO USE FOR SOULS.

One of this army of a quarter of a million women recently said to Mrs. Campbell:

"I don't see how anybody can much longer keep soul and body together."

"We don't," said one of the other women, turning suddenly. "I got rid of my soul long ago, such as it was. Who's got time to think about souls, grinding away here fourteen hours a day, to turn out contract goods? 'Tain't souls that count. It's bodies that can be driven and half starved, and driven still, till they drop in their tracks. I would try the river if I was not driving to pay a doctor's bill for my three that went with the fever. Before that I was driving to put food into their mouths. I never owed a cent to no man. I have been honest, and paid as I went, and done a good turn when I could. Had I chosen the other thing while I had a pretty face of my own, I would have had ease and comfort, and a quick death. The river's the best place

I'm thinking, for them that wants ease. Such a life as this is not living."

"She don't mean it," the first speaker said, apologetically, "she knows there are better times ahead."

"Yes, the kind you will find in the next room. Take a look in there, and then tell me what we are going to do."

In the next room was found a pantaloon maker, huddled in an old shawl, finishing the last of a dozen, which, when taken back, would give her money for fire and food. She had been ill for three days. The bed was an old mattress on a dry goods box in the corner, and save for the chair on which she sat and the stove, the room was empty.

SIXTY THOUSAND HOMELESS.

Do not believe that these are exceptional cases. They are typical specimens from the army of this dark underworld. There are 50,000 homeless men and women in the city of New York alone, an army of 50,000 that do not know where they will lay their heads to night. The other day a man in a fit of insanity murdered his wife and three children. How do we know it was insanity? They say he became a maniac. And yet the poet tells us of how the old hero, Virginius, could slay his child rather than see her dishonored. Is it not possible, in view of these frequent horrors, they have been prompted not by insanity, but by the despair of love, by the father and mother that stood on the brink and peered over the awful abyss, and preferred to kill their own, rather than to deliver them to the hell they saw open before them?

Such poverty is necessarily the mother of despair—despair grim and sullen and stupefying. The man who fights with hunger becomes an animal. Is it not better to die a man than to die a brute? Can these desperate people reason? Suicide becomes a luxury. The death of a child under such conditions is a joy, not a sorrow. They are gathered to the potter's field, but they rest. They are crowded one on top of the other in the big, black trenches, but they will not be roused in the gray twilight of the morning to dull, ceaseless toil. Their little bodies molder together in the grave, but their little stomachs do not cry for bread, and for meat and for drink. Their little faces do not grow pinched and worn any longer. There are some things worse than death. There are some things worse than the potter's field—it is the living potter's field, the living death.

THE SUBMERGED SIXTH.

In 1890 in New York City, there were 36,679 deaths: 7,059 died in the hospitals, insane asylums and work-houses. That is to say, more than one person in every six who died in this great city died in a public institution, and nearly 4,000 of those who thus died were thrown in the potter's field for burial. Talk about your "submerged tenth"! This is the "submerged sixth"! In 1894 over 5,000 people were buried in the potter's field, and of a total death-roll of 40,000, over 10,000 died in hospitals, jails, almshouses, asylums and workhouses! A submerged fourth!

It is no use to preach hell any more to the poor people of New York. They hope to better their condition in the next world, whether they go up or down. Mrs. Helen Campbell, who has spent her life among the poor of New York, says:

"We pack the poor away in tenements crowded and foul beyond anything known even to London, whose bitter cry is less yours than ours. And we have taken excellent care that no foot of ground shall remain, that means breathing space or free sport to a child, or any green growing thing. Grass pushes its way here and there, but for this army of weary workers it is only something they may lie under, never upon.

"There is no pause in the march. As one and another drops out the gap fills instantly, every alley and byway holding unending substitutes. It is not labor that profiteth, for body and soul are alike starved. It is labor in its basest and most degrading form—labor that is a curse and never a blessing, as true work may be and is. It blinds the eyes; it steals away joy; it blunts all power, whether of hope or faith; it wrecks the body and it starves the soul; it is waste and only waste. Nor can it below ground or above hold fructifying power for any human soul. It is as student, not as professional philanthropist, that I write, and the years that have brought experience, have also brought a conviction sharpened by every fresh series of facts, that no words, no matter what power of fervor may lie behind, can make plain the sorrow of the poor."

How has Protestantism in New York answered this awful cry of the lame, the blind, the deaf, the dead? By deserting their fields one by one, to build more palatial establishments in the favored spots among the houses of the rich! Is this success or failure?

CHAPTER III.

Protestantism Becoming a Bourgeois Aristocracy.

The masses of the people in New York are not in touch with Protestant church life. This is stating the case in its mildest aspect. It would be nearer the whole truth to say that the masses of the people are either alienated or hostile to our present regime of Protestantism. We have already seen by the study of church attendance, church membership and church census under the National Government that the Protestant churches cut an insignificant figure in the manhood life of New York.

This alienation and hostility are not based on antagonism to the religion of Jesus Christ. A crowd of workingmen in New York have within the past decade been known to cheer the name of Jesus, and hiss the name of the church almost in the same moment. The opposition to the church is because of its present constitution and ideal. The Protestant churches in New York to-day, as a rule, are composed too exclusively of the rich and the well to-do. A man shabbily dressed, without credentials, would be rejected as an applicant for membership, whatever might be his profession or religious experience, in the best self-supporting establishments. The question of membership is usually settled by an investigation conducted by a committee whose business it is to investigate the man's business, his standing, his motives, his prospects in this world, and his hopes for the next. This is done under the idea that only thus can the Church of God be protected from a mob of imposters. And yet the rush has not begun so far as anybody in the last century has observed. This committee is usually composed of the most bigoted men available, and under its withering influence people are being constantly driven from the doors and beyond the reach of our churches. The ideal aimed at is a high-toned social club, that shall support itself in handsome style for the benefit of its constituent members and their successors, chosen with due care. The tendency of the church is, therefore, steadily and persistently toward the creation and maintenance of a bourgeois aristocracy. This is one of the chief causes of the failure of Protestantism in New York.

THE REIGN OF THE COMMON PEOPLE.

The progress of the world is steadily and rapidly toward democracy. To-day the common people rule the world. Emperors, kings, presidents and elective representatives hold the offices, but the common people really rule already. The time will soon be upon the world when they will rule in form as well as in fact. Empires are to-day but the dungheaps out of which republics grow. The French empire was the prelude of the republic. The empire of Brazil was a fiction long before it toppled at the breath of an obscure army officer. It is doubtful if Germany sees a successor to William II. The monarchy in England is purely a popular fiction perpetuated by the historical instincts of the English people. The Queen of England has far less power than the President of the United States; her duties are purely ceremonial. The time was in our history when kings and princes filled the pages of human history. Now, the historian writes the record of the life of the common people, else it is not considered a history. The eyes of the world are on the masses. For them the scientist toils to make the forces of nature their servants. Art portrays to-day the common life of the race as its highest ideal. Literature once fawned at the feet of titled fools. Now, the literature of the race is about the common people, and it is addressed distinctly to them. Wealth even has felt this overpowering influence, is beginning to build its millions into popular colleges, circulating libraries, and public legacies and trusts. The millionaire who dies to-day, holding his millions as his own, is openly hissed while he lives, and boldly and publicly cursed while he lies cold in his coffin.

THE ETHICAL PURPOSE OF HUMANITY.

In short the ethical purpose of the humanity of the century is fixed upon the uplifting and ennobling of the masses. This is precisely the purpose of Christianity. It always has been, it always must be. It is the unfailing evidence of the presence of the true church of Jesus. Here only do we find the historic continuity of Christianity unbroken. Where is the machine called the Church to-day, and what is it about? Is its supreme purpose the saving of this dark, vulgar mass of humanity? If so, it is the true Church of Christ. Otherwise we must seek the historical continuity of Christianity outside the four walls of the institution. In short, the church that does not reach the common people, whatever it is, cannot claim to be Christian.

Christianity is not a creed, or a philosophy, or a scheme of ethics, or a theory about the universe. Christianity is Jesus Christ. It is founded upon His unique personality as the incarnation of truth, the message of God to man through man. This being true, the Church of Jesus Christ that has the right to His name must be founded on His personality. Jesus Himself was of the common people. He was of lowly birth. He was the son of the carpenter. His childhood was passed in this humble home, with its lowly surroundings. He was born poor, lived and died poor. The foxes had holes, the birds of the air nests, but He had not where to lay His head. The one title by which He loved to designate Himself was not the Son of God, but the Son of man. He mingled with the masses, taught among them, lived with them, lived for them, died for them. The Pharisaic and traditional teacher did not darken the home of the poor and outcast, but the news passed from lip to lip that the great Galilean teacher had been seen in the humblest homes, and the accusation was brought against Him that He ate with publicans and sinners. What a startling contrast is this figure of Jesus with the proud Pharisee of his day, or with the prouder Pharisee of modern times.

WHY JESUS WEPT.

The miracles of Jesus were all miracles of mercy wrought for the benefit of this great, helpless mass. We are told that He looked out upon the moving thousands as they thronged about Him, and His heart was moved with compassion. He was moved to tears as He saw them scattered as sheep without a shepherd. The first sermon that He preached was from this text: "The Lord hath anointed Me to preach the Gospel to the poor." He was popular with the masses of the people. They followed Him, they thronged Him, and His enemies did not dare molest Him during the three years of His ministry, because of their fear of the people. Again and again we are told that they did not lay hands on Him because they feared the people. I would like to know if anybody in New York would hesitate to lay hands on the average preacher for fear of the people? Upon the other hand, the people, as a rule, would gladly aid in his arrest and persecution. This is a startling fact, but it is a fact. The editors of certain papers in New York understand this only too well. Their choicest rascality is to slander and vilify Protestant ministers. The reason of it is, that the average Protestant minister finds no sympathy with the heart of the masses of the people. Hence they lie and slander, and vilify with the utmost impunity.

WHY THEY CRUCIFIED HIM.

The life of Jesus was spent in the supreme work of ministering to the needs and aspirations, the weaknesses and the sins of this dark crowd. As he passed through the country, men small of stature climbed into trees, that they might see Him and speak a message to Him as He passed. The crowds thronged Him by the sea until it was necessary to push out into a boat that He might have room to speak to them. He stood by the gates of the

A BOURGEOIS ARISTOCRACY.

city and healed the sick who were unable to find a physician. He died for them and because of them. His final arraignment of the Pharisees was the cause of His execution. From His lips, gentle with a thousand messages of love, there poured that terrific arraignment of the Scribe and Pharisee as hypocrites and sons of hell. His words cut to the very marrow of the bone. They could not forgive Him. They determined to use all their power to destroy Him and they succeeded in accomplishing His downfall. But when He died the last vestige of the traditionalism which separated the people from the God of the people, was destroyed. The veil of the temple was rent in twain, and the holy of holies laid bare, so that the great mass who had not dared to look upon the shining altar, save through the person of the high priest, were now invited to come boldly into the presence of their father, their friend, and make every want, every wish, every aspiration known. The last commission of Jesus Christ was worldwide. The doctrine of election which He taught was the election of His people to a purpose, and that purpose was the salvation of the world. "Go," was His command, "Go into all the world, preach the Gospel to the whole creation."

ONLY CLASS NOT A CLASS.

The objective of Christianity being the salvation of the whole world, it is impossible to construct a church with this purpose that does not reach, and seek as an end to reach, the masses, simply because the history of the masses is the history of the world. Outside of the history of the common people, there is nothing worth relating. They are not a class. They are the people. They are mankind. They are the only so-called class that are not a class. The history of a state, of a nation, of an age, is simply the story of the life of the common people. To reach them and to save them is to reach and save the world. To fail to reach them is to lose the world. In this dark, vulgar mass lies the destiny of the race. I said that the other classes are as nothing. This may seem an exaggeration, and yet it is not. The calculations of different astronomers give a variation of about a million miles in distance from the earth to the sun, and yet this variation of a million miles is so insignificant in the calculation of the movement of the planets, that it may be thrown aside as a fraction that does not interfere with the final results, and it is possible to calculate the time of an eclipse one hundred years from to-day with either one of these computations of the sun's distance. So in the history of mankind. We may throw aside a few million people, who are out of the current of the great masses, as unworthy of consideration in computing the final result. In the arithmetic of the universe, a million men, more or less, who belong to a special class, have no appreciable effect in the grand total of world destinies.

THE DREGS AND FROTH OF LIFE.

Not to be of the masses is to be out of touch with the race. I am sorry for the poor, feeble-minded man who is anxious to trace his ancestry in a direction that avoids the great stream of the race. Human society constantly sluffs at both ends—the dregs at one end, the froth at the other. The upper crust is as much a nuisance in its way, as the dregs which fall to the bottom, and the man who aspires to be of the froth is in the last analysis no better than he who supinely sinks with the dregs. There are many who aspire mightily to enter a select circle of so-called high society. And yet I read the other day of a great whiskered babe in this charmed circle, who was thirty summers of age, and yet such a baby that he could not enter upon the daring work of self-propagation without assistance. All the world's great men have come from the masses of the people. There is not a man whose name is worth the thought of the world for an hour who did not come from the masses. We readily understand, therefore, the ideal of Jesus when He wrought among the masses. He sought to leaven the whole human race. He therefore planted his leaven in the midst of the lump. It was not an accident that Jesus Christ, the incarnate Son of God, **was the son** of a carpenter. It was not a blunder of God Almighty that this thing happened. It was a part of His plan of world redemption conceived in completeness before the morning of creation. To learn thoroughly this secret is to probe to the depth of the mission of Christ. Here His Church must come to learn the ways by which it is to reach and save men. When with open hearts we grasp this ministry of humility in the incarnation, we have touched the inmost secret of the Heart of Christ and of the Father.

THE PROTESTANT EPISCOPAL CHURCH'S LAST OPPORTUNITY.

There was a time in the history of the Episcopal Church when, if its leaders had had the breadth of heart and the wisdom and foresight needed for the hour, they could have made the Church of England the Church of the English speaking race for all time; but they refused to understand John Wesley. They refused to open the doors of the church that it might receive this vulgar mass, toward whom his heart went out in undying love and sympathy. The Episcopal Church lost here an opportunity of the ages. The question now arises, what church will have the wisdom, the foresight, the love, to readjust itself in this twentieth century that is coming to the world needs of the people? The church that does will be the true church of Christ, and in His name will conquer.

HEAVEN THE HOME OF THE MASSES.

Heaven is the home of the redeemed millions. The Book declares, "Straight is the gate and narrow is the way that leads to heaven; and wide is the gate and broad the way that leads to destruction." We are told that this is an indication that few will be saved and many lost. Nothing could be further from the truth. Jesus was here describing the condition of the world at the moment He spoke. He had no earthly reference to the end of time and the final results. Hear the magnificent shout of the Apocalyptic seer as he looked at the end of time, "And I saw a great multitude, which no man could number, stretching away from the throne out into the blue of heavens, with its countless hosts lost amid the clouds; from every nation, and every race, and every country, and every tribe, and every tongue." This is the glimpse of heaven given to the seer. No, if you wish to avoid the crowd, if you desire to keep out of the rush, you will have to go to the other place. Hell will be the home of the select few. I do not say that all the upper ten are going to hell. Far from it. But I do say that many of this circle, as now constituted, are certainly in a fair way to get there; and I am sure of one thing, that the man who is uncomfortable in a crowd will not find heaven to his taste.

A PRIVATE PEW.

I was talking with the conductor of a Pullman car on my way South from Washington the other day, and this conductor told me something of his life. He said that some years ago he was a desperate young man. He came to himself and realized his situation and determined that he would be a better man. He determined to find the truth of religion and walk in that way. When he reached Washington he sought out at once the church of his father and mother and entered, determining in his heart to find the light if he could. He took a seat in the church, and he said he had not remained more than a few minutes when an usher came up and said to him, "You cannot sit in this seat; it is a private pew and is taken." The young man replied, "Very well, I will vacate it as soon as the owners appear." The usher replied: "No, you must get up at once. We do not allow people to occupy the pews before the owners appear." "Well," said the young man, "have you no pews for visitors?" "No," replied the usher, "the seats are all taken by regular pewholders." So, accompanied by the usher, the young man said he arose and marched down the aisle and out of the church. "And when I reached the lobby," said he, "I turned to that usher and said, 'You go to your preacher and tell him that he can take his pulpit and his pews, and his sexton and his ushers and his people and go to hell. I will never cross the threshold of a church of this faith again if I live to be a hundred years old.'" And he did not, though he married a wife who was a member of that church. He sought fellowship with another denomination with open doors and became the teacher of a large class of noble young men. Where there is one church with this spirit outside of New York you find two in New York. It is a peculiarity of our swell metropolitan church life.

I do not say that such churches do no good. Sometimes they do a little good. I heard the other day of one that did. A woman had tried in vain for years to get her husband to go to church. At last on one beautiful Sabbath morning she overpersuaded him and he went. When he looked around in church and saw how much more handsomely all the other women were dressed than his own wife, he was cut to the heart as he looked at her shabby clothes. When he went back home he handed her $500, and told her to buy some clothes. I am not saying that these churches are utterly sterile of good, they do sometimes accomplish such results and they are to be commended for such good works. But if we look for an institution here whose mission is to lift man from the ditch and save him, we shall be bitterly disappointed.

I say, therefore, unhesitatingly that the Christian church that does not seek to reach the masses is a humbug. It reaches nobody. It is a caricature, it is a farce, it is a swindle. In my soul of souls I believe it is a stench in the nostrils of the Father of humanity. The sooner such churches are torn down and ground into concrete the better—the better for the church, the better for truth, the better for organic religion, the better for man. Such churches, as social clubs for the exchange of social courtesies, might result in good, but, standing as the pretended embodiment of the regenerating spirit of the God, they cumber the ground. The sooner we learn this the better.

THE SKELETON HAND.

Now and then some of our big churches have a spasm of high purpose. What is the result? They build a mission. That is, they build a kitchen for their parlor and make it the receptacle, as far as possible, of the disagreeable elements in the parent establishment. Or they declare free seats for an evening service which none of their members, who have any standing in the church or polite society, ever attend. Or they may construct a free soup house on a back street somewhere. Bah! The people who are not paupers and loafers spit on such invitations as an insult. They are an insult. The strong man curses them, and the timid gives them a wide berth. I read the other day in the "Youth's Companion" a story of a well known public man who is remarkably lean and almost cadaverous. He was in the back room of a doctor's office one day, when a newsboy opened the door and shouted: "Evening paper?" "No," said the doctor, "but the man in the next room will buy one." The boy turning the knob of the door to which the doctor had pointed, opened a closet in which hung a huge skeleton. With a shriek of horror, he dashed out into the entry and ran down the stairs. The great man, entering the room, heard of the doctor's prank, and thinking it a mean trick, opened the window and told the boy he would buy a paper. The newsboy, glancing suspiciously at the thin, bony figure in the window, called back: "No, you don't! You can't fool me, if you have got your clothes on." This is just the feeling that comes over the timid when the skeleton hand of the soup kitchen edition of the church is extended to them.

An aristocracy may have had its mission in the history of man, but the life of Jesus Christ ushered in the era of the brotherhood of man. Christianity is the organization simply of this brotherhood, so far as it is an institution at all. To fail to grasp this idea is to totally misconceive the purpose of Him who said specifically, "Call no man rabbi, for all ye are brethren."

CHAPTER IV.
The Church of Christ a Democracy.

Government is the rock on which all Western Christendom has split. Democracy is the ultimate principle in the evolution of government. No serious student of human history, honest with himself and honest with the facts, can doubt this. Democracy therefore must be the goal toward which all government tends, civil or ecclesiastical. I believe this because I am a Christian. The principles of democracy are fundamental to the Christian religion. The language of Jesus Christ is on this point direct. The record declares that He called His Disciples unto Him and said: Ye know that the rulers of the Gentiles lord it over them, and their great ones exercise authority over them. Not so shall it be among you: but whosoever would become great among you shall become your minister, and whosoever would be first among you shall be your servant; even as the Son of Man came not to be ministered unto, but to minister, and to give His life a ransom for many. As the Father hath sent Me even so send I you. Be not ye called rabbi, for one is your teacher, and all ye are brethren. And call no man your father on the earth, for one is your Father which is in heaven. Neither be ye called masters, for one is your Master, even the Christ. But he that is greatest among you shall be your servant. And whosoever shall exalt himself shall be humbled, and whosoever shall humble himself shall be exalted.

If we accept the New Testament as the authoritative statement of the foundation, we must believe that the Church of Jesus Christ is a pure democracy, the grounds of whose citizenship are the alienable rights of a common brotherhood.

I believe that the Church of Christ in its truth and purity will ultimately conquer the world. If so it must represent in its governing polity the principles of pure democracy. I believe that the Church itself is simply the local assembly of God's people. I believe that in them vests the inalienable right to think for themselves, to work out their own salvation, to worship God according to the dictates of their own conscience—that is, in spirit and in truth.

"The Kingdom of God cometh not with observation," says Christ. That is, it is not from without. It is not a temporal force. He did not claim for it temporal authority. He distinctly repudiated every effort of His Disciples to set up a temporal authority, declaring on such occasions, "My kingdom is not of this world," meaning a world of human authority. The only Church to which He promised special power was the local assembly of believers. "Where two or three are met together, there am I in the midst, and that to bless." This local assembly was the only Apostolic Church of which we have any authentic record.

A BOOK SUPPRESSED.

"The Bampton Lectures" for 1888, delivered by Edwin Hatch, were suppressed in England by authority. These lectures were entitled, "The Organization of the Early Christian Churches." The reason why these lectures were suppressed was because they destroyed the foundations on which certain ecclesiastical authority had been reared in modern times. The more thorough becomes our knowledge of the ancient church the more simple becomes its organization, and the less pretense we have for our claim to any temporal authority established by Christ. The only authority recognized by Jesus in the establishment of His Church was spiritual. Here He gave unlimited power. In His promises of dominion over evil the faith of His Disciples was tested to its supreme limit. Upon every occasion that His Disciples sought the exercise of temporal authority over each other or over others they met with a rebuke whose emphasis could not be misunderstood. When they were disputing as to who should be the first in the knigdom—meaning the temporal kingdom they supposed Christ about to establish—He took a little child and put it in the midst of them, and told them that unless they became as little children they themselves could have no part in His kingdom.

POLITICS AMONG THE APOSTLES.

The mother of the sons of Zebedee with the sons came to Jesus, as He proceeds to Jerusalem at the close of His ministry, and petitions Him to clothe her children with authority over the other disciples and over His kingdom. If Jesus had meant to establish any sort of an ecclesiastical, authoritative machine, here was certainly the hour in which He would have given indication of that fact. If such had been His intention, this petition was not unreasonable. James and John were of the three who stood on the mount with Jesus and witnessed His transfiguration. They were among the favored ones of the twelve. John was the disciple specially loved by Christ. Yet what is His answer to this petition?

In the midst of the indignation of the Disciples, when they had heard the request, He calls them aside and delivers to them His emphatic message. Said Jesus: "The Gentiles exercise temporal authority over each other. They lord it over one another. They have temporal rulers that are called princes and benefactors. It shall not be so with you. The way to preferment in my kingdom is the way of the cross, is the way of sacrifice, the way of service. If any man would be first let him be the slave of others."

NOT TO DOMINATE BUT TO DIE.

The mission of Jesus Christ was not to rule, but to serve. "The Son of Man came not to be ministered unto, but to minister." The mission of Jesus Christ was not to dominate, but to die, "and to give His life a ransom for many." Over the powers of evil in things spiritual Christ's gift of authority was simply boundless. Upon His Church He bestowed the authority spiritual to forgive sins through the proclamation of the Gospel, to bind and to loose. Here His Disciples' faith could not rise to the limit of their privileges, but it was constantly necessary for Him to rebuke their aspirations for temporal power, wherein they misunderstood His mission on earth.

PARENTAL AUTHORITY.

Democracy is the only form of church government that can possibly be harmonized at last with the fundamental truths taught by Jesus. His doctrine of God calls for such a polity. He came to reveal God as the Father universal. He came to declare the Father. He taught the world to pray "Our Father." The authority of a father is a power that cannot be delegated. It is in the blood. He declared the government of God to be parental, the government of His Church to be parental, with the Parent in heaven, the family on earth bound together by the common ties of an equal brotherhood. His doctrine of man necessitates the acceptance of the principles of free government.

A CHILD OF THE KING.

Jesus declared man to be a child of God. A child of the King in whose veins flow the royal blood of the King. Jesus declared the intrinsic divinity of man as man set forth his immortal worth, his immortal capacities, his immortal destiny, his immortal rights. He came to die not for kings and princes and nobles and those who moved in the high circles of society—he died for man—man in the ditch, man in the gutter, man in the highway robber, man in every grade of degradation and sin. He declared that man was in himself, of himself, worthy of the supremest sacrifice of God in love on his behalf. He taught the human race—all nations, all races, all kindred, all tribes, all classes—to look up into the heavens and to say, "Our Father." When He taught the world this lesson He threw around the race the golden chord of an universal, fraternal bond. He proclaimed the equality of man; equality in fraternity. He declared that in His kingdom there should be no lording over each other, because they were all brethren. Titles and class distinctions He declared to belong to the unregenerate world--the world that was to pass away and bow at last to His universal empire.

FIRST CHURCH SCANDAL.

The ultimate outcome of every departure from the basis of fraternal democracy in the history of the church has resulted in evil and disgrace.

The first church scandal in sacred history before the death of Christ, was this disgraceful attempt of certain disciples to obtain temporal authority over their brethren.

As we come down to the centuries after Christ, we find, without an exception, that the darkest pages in the history of Christianity have been those on which men have written the history of their ambitions for power. The disgraces of church history are indelibly traced to the determination of men to rule over their fellow-men, to dictate to them what they shall believe, and what they shall do, and how they shall worship God.

THUMBSCREW, RACK, TORCH.

The history of the thumbscrew is the history of this daring assumption of power which Christ denied to His Church. The history of the wheel, of the rack, of the torch, of the inquisition, of the massacres that disgraced the name of historic Christianity, are all traceable to this attempt to establish within the church what Jesus distinctly declared should not enter it. The disgraceful perversion of truth in the sale of indulgences, which led in the Catholic Church to the Reformation, is directly to be traced to this fundamental error of delegated authority temporal on earth.

Here we find the stumbling-blocks in the way of the Church to-day in its progress, Catholic as well as Protestant. The stumbling-blocks to-day in the way of the Protestant church we find to be the pitiful squabbles over ecclesiastical definitions, passwords and authorities. Whenever the church sets up its claim to ecclesiastical power on earth, it is certain to reach at last absurd lengths that lead only to disgrace and the perversion of the fundamental principles of Christianity.

A PASS TO HEAVEN.

A curious illustration of the development of this idea of authority was recently given in Russia, and we are still in the Russian stage of religion. The young Grand Duchess Paul recently died. Before the coffin was closed, the metropolitan put a written paper in the right hand of the corpse, which read as follows: "We, by the grace of God, prelate of the holy Russian Church, write this to our master and friend, St. Peter, the gatekeeper of the Lord Almighty. We announce to you that the servant of the Lord, her imperial highness, the Grand Duchess Paul, has finished her life on earth, and we order you to admit her into the kingdom of heaven without delay, for we have absolved all her sins and granted her salvation. You will obey our order on sight of this document, which we put into her hand." The grand duchess was buried and the worms destroyed the paper. Where is the grand duchess?

THE CROSS AND DEMOCRACY

As the church attains its true work and position, the policy of fraternal democracy must become more and more its working basis. The first democracies in the history of the world were built on the principles of Christianity. There were no democracies before Christ. Greece and Rome were not democracies. They were not even republics. The Grecian world, when Greece ruled the world, was divided into two classes—Greeks and barbarians. The barbarian had no rights. He was a brute, the beast of burden for the oligarchy that called itself Grecian. When Rome was mistress of the world the world was divided into two classes—Roman citizens and slaves. The slaves were butchered for the Roman populace. It remained for the principles of Christianity to work out in the history of the world the first democracies we have ever known. The history of the cross has been the centre around which has clustered the fight for human freedom. The cross of Jesus Christ has been the advance herald of liberty, equality, fraternity. Wherever the principles of Christianity were taught, class distinctions were undermined at their very foundation. As the Kingdom of Christ progresses, all such artificial distinctions must at last be destroyed.

TRIUMPHANT DEMOCRACY.

The American nation pre-eminently is Christian in its foundations. Its Declaration of Independence and its Constitutions are but paraphrases of the principles taught by Jesus Christ, and taught by Him in the history of the world. Democracy is the first manifest destiny of the world. The movement of the race towards this ultimate principle of government is resistless. It is a race movement. It is an age movement. It is a movement limited, however, in the history of the world, to the bounds of Christian civilization. The world has no history outside of Christian civilization to-day. The American democracy is but little over a hundred years old, and yet witness the result! Lift your eye and look to the north, the south, the east, the west, and to-day there remains on this vast continent not a single crowned head. Crowns, thrones, scepters, titles, classes are doomed. They belong to a past that is yielding to a future holding in its hands the dominating principles of truth.

THE GOOD IN SLAVERY.

If you ask the question, Has not the assumption of authority by men, specially qualified as kings and nobles and rulers, been beneficial to men in the history of the world? I answer, Yes, often this has been true. Take for instance the institution of slavery. Slavery has its beneficent aspect. I honestly believe that when the history of slavery in the Southern States shall be written a hundred years from now, when passions and prejudices shall have passed away, the historian will find that the beneficent aspects of slavery in the South were far larger than the world suspects to-day. The South lifted the African from the bondage of savagery into the light and strength of Christian-civilization. He lifted him at a bound across the chasm of centuries. Yet while this is true, I thank God that there is not to-day the clang of a single slave's chain on this continent. Slavery may have had its beneficent aspects, but democracy is the destiny of the race, because all men are bound together in the bonds of fraternal equality with one common Father above.

A TRAGEDY IN TRADITION.

Institutions that were of use in the past will have no place in the history of the future. They may have belonged to the condition of infancy of the race, but have no part in the story of the race's manhood. Out in Kansas recently there lived an old grandfather ninety years old, with his son and granddaughter. The granddaughter was taken ill with the grip. The old grandfather had been a physician in his time in an Eastern village. He tried all his mild remedies in vain and finally came to the conclusion that bleeding was necessary. The father refused to permit the experiment, but while he was away the old man persuaded the girl to let him try taking a little blood from her arm. In his feeble hand the knife slipped, and the brachial artery was severed. The grandfather tried in vain to stem the flow of blood. When the father returned, he found his daughter dead and his father by her side in a swoon. The poor old man could not rally from the terrible shock and soon died. The old doctor may have had his uses once with his lancet. I fear his real usefulness depended more on the imagination of his patient than on the realities of good in his remedies. Whatever may have been his uses in the past, he belongs to an era from which the world, as the world is free, is delivered. The cry "Back to the old paths!" is the feeble rallying call of a reminiscent senility.

The church must either lead or be led in this world movement of the race. We are now in the first years of the reign of the common people. Power has been gradually descending or ascending, as you may like, from the head of king and prince and aristocrat, until the crown of empire rests upon the head of the everyday unit of society. Science bends its energy toward discovering the secrets of nature that will make the life of the masses richer and better. History now records not the life of kings and princes and armies, but tells us the story of the everyday life of the common people. The eyes of the world are on the great undermasses. The church that holds the ideal of a decaying aristocracy in this age, is calling upon a dead past to save from the resistless avalanche of a new world life.

CHAPTER V.

Sectarianism.

Sectarianism is the personal equation in religion. As many men so many minds. Grant to these men religious liberty, and their division along the lines of personal sympathies, tastes and antipathies will be certain. In this sense, sectarianism has a true mission to fulfil for man. In its true development it should mean liberty in non-essentials, diversity within a great unity.

The denial of liberty in the past has been the potent cause of the strife and bloodshed that has disgraced the record of historic Christianity.

Uniformity gained by force does not mean unity. The belief that it does is the one tragic superstition of our history. To preserve this "unity" of the Jewish religion the constituted authorities crucified Jesus Christ. Such is the record of the thumbscrew, the rack, the wheel, the torch. This spirit drenched England in blood, bathed the world in Huguenot tears, sent Alva into the Netherlands to butcher 18,000 victims in six years, and in Protestant history burned Servetus in the Old World, the witches in New England, and imprisoned and whipped the Baptists in Virginia. The best definition, therefore, of a saint ever made is "One cannonaded while living; canonized when dead."

Man can only see anything through the medium of his own personality. The captain of a river steamer was recently received in to the church of his choice. He was a man of energy. They made him an officer. Soon after his election, he heard one day that there was a leak in the church. He promptly went to the building, took a lantern and went down into the cellar to locate it. From what other point of view could a sailor look for a leak?

There are no two leaves alike; no two trees alike. Nature duplicates nothing. And her life is one! Infinite diversity in a great unity.

It is just beginning to dawn on the Christian world that this is a possibility. But the dawn slowly breaks. When the Sun of love and liberty rises, one of the chief causes of our stumbling will be removed.

We have much zeal and sacrifice in New York, but as yet it takes the form of the emphasis of small differences into abnormalities. It is sectarian zeal rather than Christian. Many of our leading pastors wear out their shoes and their souls running after their own members to keep them out of the church of a zealous rival around the corner.

The Presbyterians established a successful mission work in Persia. When its success was observed the Episcopal Church sent over its "priests" to tell these deluded people that they had received a spurious brand of Christianity, and that the only genuine article bore their trade-mark, duly copyrighted and protected by a legislature that had adjourned *sine die* centuries ago and never met since. Congregationalism holds New England and Presbyterians now are establishing missions in New England to save their people from the damnation of error. In New York's richest and most prosperous districts, where churches are least needed, we have the most shameful and senseless crowding of Protestant churches, where fundamental differences are nothing.

Nine-tenths of the doctrines of all the denominations of Christendom are one—Roman Catholic and Protestant. We believe in one God—manifesting himself as Father, Son, Spirit.

We believe that we have salvation only in Christ.

Our songs are one. Toplady and Wesley were violently antagonistic in the definition of theology, but we all sing "Rock of Ages" and "Jesus, Lover of My Soul." Newman was a Roman Catholic Cardinal, but we all sing "Lead Kindly Light." The author of "In the Cross of Christ I Glory" and "Nearer My God to Thee" was a Unitarian. But we all sing their songs, and our heart life is one!

SECTARIANISM.

In ethics, the Christian world is one. Love to God and love to man, and the Ten Commandments are the ethical code of Christendom.

Our divisions are on stupid trifles. The smaller the difference, the fiercer the conflict.

The old councils wrestled for days over petty differences of opinion on the details of theological science, and occasionally the Bishops kicked each other to death by way of argument.

The Greek and the Latin Churches are separated by fewer differences than any other, and yet they are the widest apart. The Pope and the Czar are implacable foes and eternal rivals. The unspeakable Turk stands guard with his musket to keep Greek and Latin priests from tearing each other to pieces over the tomb of Jesus during Passion week!

The effects of the sectarian method are everywhere apparent in the centres of our modern life, and nowhere so painfully as in New York. The consequence is that just those fields whose needs are most painful are those invariably deserted in the sectarian scramble for the best positions. One million four hundred thousand people in New York live in second and third-class tenements. There are districts of 50,000 of these people without a single church of any sort among them! The scramble for choice corner lots in the favored districts continues unabated. Imagine, if you can, a consultation among the Apostles on the subject of real estate in Jerusalem and Rome for church sites. Imagine, if you can, St. Peter describing with eloquence, a choice bit of ground on a new avenue, soon to be peopled by the very rich merchants whose caravans brought in daily the treasures of the heathen world.

The waste of men, zeal and money in the senseless duplication of Protestant Churches in communities where they are not needed, is something appalling. It is estimated by a careful church statistician, who has made a detailed study of the subject, that there are 25,000 such Protestant churches in America.

that have no reason for their existence. More than $12,500,000 are locked up in these dead plants. It is a crime.

In division and fight there is always weakness. Whenever the men who conduct any great business begin to fight themselves, forthwith the business is mixed. It does not matter how ancient and honorable the establishment, it must go down in a factional fight. This law is absolutely without exception. In one sense the visible church is a business establishment, and its affairs must be conducted on business principles. Some years ago the country was crazy on the subject of baseball. Thousands of people crowded the fields to witness this truly national amusement. The baseball people began to fight among themselves and their successes. We had the senseless duplication of buildings and grounds at enormous expense. They fought each other in the newspapers. Then the public quit the habit of baseball and went back to its business, and there was a season of wrecks and assignments and reorganization.

Recently the American public were crazy on yachts and yachting. The rage continued until the big yachtsmen began to quarrel. Whereupon the people quit reading about yachts and turned their attention to other things. This has been precisely the effect of our senseless and extravagant wars with one another in the religious world. I wonder when it will cease and we will grant each other the right to differ on small things and yet work together as one man to accomplish the great thing—the salvation of man.

CHAPTER VI.

Dead Theologies.

Theology is a science. Religion is a life. The one is an analysis, the other a fact. Theology therefore must always express itself in the terms of the knowledge of the age. It bears the same relation to religion that the science of physiology bears to the body. The old physiologists knew nothing about the circulation of the blood, or the nervous system. Each new discovery enlarges by so much the science which was its expression. Astronomy has grown as our knowledge of the heavens has expanded from year to year. We welcome every new discovery and add it to the sum of our knowledge with gratitude to God. The unique feature about the science of theology is that many of its professors deny the possibility of enlargement. The human race has grown from infancy to mature manhood; the knowledge of the world has been increased every hour of its history—and yet theologians insist that theology is a mummy and a mummy it shall ever remain The stage-coach yielded to the vestibuled limited, the sailing vessel to the ocean greyhound, but theology rakes up the ashes of a dead past and weeps over the grave of Adam. We are solemnly informed that the minds of the long past centuries only could comprehend and express truth. We are commanded to learn the science of theology only from the ages in which the science of medicine consisted in bleeding; chemistry was a black art, astronomy the profession of a fakir, and electricity was regarded as a manifestation of the devil or the shekina of God! Knowledge is the inheritance of all mankind except the preacher. He must not taste of the tree of knowledge under penalty of death.

PROGRESS AND STAGNATION.

In 1840 a young Irishman was sent to the New York penitentiary for life for killing a man in a drunken frenzy. He was pardoned some time ago by the governor. He emerged from the prison a grey-haired, bent old man. The world was new to him. He walked the streets of New York in unceasing wonder. He gazed upon the Brooklyn Bridge as though it were a miracle. The towering fifteen story building seemed about to topple and crush him. What a different world it was from the one he knew fifty years ago. New York had grown from a town of 300,000 inhabitants to the huge metropolis, the centre of 3,000,000 of people, the second city of the civilized world. Human slavery had been abolished, and the nation, baptized in blood, had risen to a new life. The German Empire had been created; the maps of the world made over again. Steam had been practically applied to travel and the face of the earth transformed. There were no more seas. Liverpool had been brought nearer to New York than San Francisco. The telegraph had made the world a whispering gallery, and the cylinder printing press universal education a fact, not a dream; while the dynamo had crowned the brow of humanity with a coronet of light. He gazed upon a new world. Old things had passed away. But had he examined the Protestant churches of New York he would have found but one serious change, and that geographical—they had moved uptown! Their theology shows no growth—their methods are the methods used by their fathers and their grandfathers, in this age of progress, a solecism—stupid, irrational, immoral!

HOMES FOR THE AGED.

The results of this method were inevitable. The men who have made this age the miracle of history soon learn to treat the church with contempt. They leave it to the women and children and go about the more serious work of life—that life whose activities involve the progress of the human race, that life of reality in which deeds are the only creeds that are worthy of notice. Hence the Protestant churches become more and more simply homes for the aged, the infirm, the feeble minded, the griefs of widowhood and kindergarten for children young and old.

The essence of Protestantism is the rebellion of the reason against the shackles of a mechanical "authority." Protestantism, with conscience fettered by tradition, stultifies its own life and has no reason for its existence. Protestantism, because of its very nature, must go forward or die. There is a tendency even in great minds to grow weary and stop in their upward march, become traditionalists and reactionaries. Find this where you will it means decay. Even Daniel Webster illustrates this truth.

In 1838, Daniel Webster, our greatest constitutional lawyer, said on the floor of the United States Senate, in opposition to a measure then before Congress to establish a post route from Independence, Mo., to the mouth of the Columbia River: "What do we want with this vast worthless area? This region of savages and wild beasts, of deserts, shifting sands and whirlwinds of dust, of cactus and prairie dogs? To what use could we ever hope to put these great deserts, or these endless mountain ranges, impregnable and covered to their very base with eternal snow? What can we ever hope to do with the Western coast? A coast of three thousand miles, rockbound, cheerless, uninviting, and not a harbor in it! What use have we for such a country? Mr. President, I will never vote one cent from the public treasury to place the Pacific coast one inch nearer Boston than it now is."

But there were found younger spirits willing to make the rash experiment. In 1894 Colorado produced $11,000,000 in gold and $14,000,000 in silver. The city of Denver has 160,000 inhabitants, and its smooth pavements flash daily with 20,000 bicycles. And what would California, with its tons of gold and silver and millions of tons of golden fruit, and its great shipyards say to-day to this polished effort of the great constitutional lawyer! Where one obstacle is thrown in the way of material progress, a hundred barriers are erected before the pioneer of theology. He is not only opposed—he is cursed, hounded, persecuted, excommunicated! Although New York is the centre of our progressive life, no man has dared to brook the traditions of the elders in the world of theology without having the hounds set on his trail.

The answer to any aggressive movement has been "Back to the old paths!" Are these traditionalists and reactionaries worthy of leadership? What is their history? Every step in the progress of the race toward freedom and light has been fought, inch by inch, with this old enemy of knowledge. The superstition that seeks to limit the horizon of the human soul within the bounds of personal or ancestral traditions has ever been, and is to-day, one of the deadliest foes with which the hopes of man ever contended. It seems utterly preposterous that in this enlightened age, here in New York City, the centre of free thought for a new world, we should have to-day the narrowest and most bigoted ecclesiasticism.

HERESY! HERESY!

Yet it is so. One hundred and sixteen clergymen of the Episcopal Church that recently made overtures to the Christian world for church union fiercely demand the scalps of two of her mightiest men for daring to invite the ministers of other Christian bodies to speak to their people at a special Friday evening service! Our good Presbyterian brethren also demanded the head of Prof. Briggs in a charger because he had been guilty of the crime of thinking, and worse still, of giving utterance to his thoughts. These men invariably change their tactics during the progress of the battle they hasten to join. They first call to war with a whoop— with a mighty noise—with a great hoot! They next declare in the fiercest language that the Bible is being destroyed. Then in a little while after they have crucified some of God's noblest servants, they all solemnly protest that in reality they always held the same doctrine! They then blow their noses, scent the air for a new trail, and whet their jaw bones for another conflict in new fields.

I fearlessly maintain that the men who have been the champions of the forms and traditions of ecclesiasticism have ever been, and are to-day, the deadliest enemies of true Christianity.

They have systematically repressed, crucified or destroyed the personality of the noblest ministers of truth.

CHRIST A HERETIC.

These are the men who crucified the Christ. They slew Him because He kept not the word of the elders. They hated Him because He emphasized the truth that God is spirit and they that worship Him must worship in spirit and in truth. He set at naught their ecclesiastical tom-foolery and plainly told them that they were whited sepulchres—hypocrites who could not escape the damnation of hell. Theirs was the most constant, persistent, dogged and utterly devilish opposition Jesus encountered. They followed Him like hounds. They asked Him cunningly devised questions to convict Him of heterodoxy. They tried to catch Him in His words. They accused Him of eating with unwashed hands. They accused Him of breaking the Sabbath. They declared that He ate with sinners. They said He was the friend of publicans and harlots. He did all these things, He was all these things, plainly telling them that He came not to call the righteous, but sinners. When at last they despaired of binding his divine personality with the chains of their traditions, they slew Him. They flapped their sable wings, called their council under cover of the night, condemned Him to death for heresy, dragged Him up Calvary's hill, and crucified Him, mocking and saying: "He saved others! Himself He cannot save!"

Since the crucifixion these men who have been busy keeping the traditions of the elders have continued bravely their work of destroying the divinest personalities among the servants of truth. Traditionalism stoned Stephen to death. Traditionalism slew the Apostles. Traditionalism has been busy with red

DEAD THEOLOGIES.

hands, butchering the Lord's anointed down to the latest generation of the nineteenth century.

JOHN WESLEY, "A LIAR."

Canon Farrar says of John Wesley: "The most simple, the most innocent, the most generous of men, he was called a liar, an immoral and designing intriguer, a pope, a Jesuit, a swindler, the most notorious hypocrite living. The clergy, I grieve to say, led the way. Rowland Hill called Wesley a lying apostle, a designing wolf, a dealer in stolen wares, and said that he was as unprincipled as a rook, and as silly as jackdaw, first pilfering his plumage, and then going proudly forth to display it to a laughing world. The revival of religion had to make its way among hostile bishops, furious controversialists, jibing and libellous newspapers, angry men of the world, prejudiced juries, and brutal lies. And yet it prevailed, because one with God is always in a majority.

CHOKED TO DEATH.

They have choked them to death with orthodox iron collars forged around their young necks in their preliminary training. Many of these traditional institutions advertise their shops with the boast that their collars are warranted to hold for time and eternity; that if a man remains long enough to fix it firmly about his neck, he is certain to think only in one set groove, and then only to a limited degree. When the men begin to grow, the collar never grows. It was not made to grow. Inflammation sets in. The man either breaks the collar or chokes to death. To break the collar is a very painful operation. The flesh has grown to it and all around it. Besides, if he persists in breaking the collar the traditionalists who forged it proceed to do their best to break his neck before it has time to get new strength in freedom. Thousands of men allow themselves to be choked gradually to death rather than enter on the painful struggle, and perhaps get their necks broken. They smother the best ministers to death. Smother them to death with the old, worm-eaten mantles that some good men of another generation wore. David, "when he had served his generation, fell on sleep." But these men insist that the generation of the past, not the generation of the present, be served. Some of the best preachers ever called to this city have been smothered to death because traditionalists have heaped upon them the worn-out rubbish of former ages. These traditionalists are not altogether heartless. They have feeling. They weep mightily over the fall of Adam, while the children of Adam stumble over them into hell. They are too busy weeping over the grave of Adam to pay any attention to his children. Besides, they take refuge in the consoling doctrine of predestined damnation and election, and give free course to their historic and ancient grief.

FLAME, SWORD, THUMBSCREW, RACK

Traditionalists have heaped upon the church of Christ the infamy of a history of cruelty and inhumanity, of flame and sword, thumbscrew, rack and torch.

Ecclesiastical Christianity is one thing, the Christianity of Christ another thing. These two things are no more alike than blood and milk. The bloodiest pages in the history of the human race have been those written by the merciless hand of the traditionalist. Tradition sent Alva into the Netherlands to ravage with a storm of fire and blood, and disgrace the name of humanity in the sacred name of Christ. Tradition revoked the edict of Nantes, until the soil of France was drunk with the blood of her children. Tradition, breathing the breath of hell, led the trembling sons and daughters of faith, barefooted and blindfolded, over burning plowshares, stretched them upon the wheel and rack, tore them limb from limb, sparing not for the groan of age, the cry of motherhood, or the lisp of childhood. With hellish glee they kindled the martyrs' fires, and danced with joy at the sight of roasting flesh.

Tradition with holy zeal hunts the Anabaptists like wild

DEAD THEOLOGIES.   65

beasts, and on the shore of a new world burns people at the stake in New England and lays the lash on the Baptist in Virginia. The Bible they have made a bludgeon with which to brain heretics. Its word they have forged into chains. Its leaves they have used as fuel to kindle martyr fires.

CRIMINAL STUPIDITY.

With unfathomable stupidity these men have persisted in arraigning the reason, the heart and the knowledge of the race against Jesus Christ and his religion.

They have assaulted science and set back the progress of the world for generations at a time. Science is the revealer of God in nature. They have sought to put out the light of science in the name of God. They stretched Galileo on the rack because he invented the telescope and discovered the laws of God and the heavens. They tortured him in the name of the God whom he was serving. For giving wings to his thoughts and soaring amid the elements to find God, they burned Bruno. When William Carey, the apostle of modern missions, rose tremblingly and gave voice to the great love that burned in his soul for the heathen world, tradition, with utmost dignity, thundered, "sit down, young man."

In the name of a God of a human made orthodoxy, they have dethroned reason, crowned and canonized stupidity. In other words, they have insisted on making a puerile system of human dogmatism the infallible guide of thought. They have set the bounds beyond which the mind of man shall not dare even think. They insist that the very language of this human dogmatism that smells of the dust and rubbish of the Dark Ages, shall be considered divine and infallible. The errors, controversies, absurdities and ignorance of the past they insist shall be now held sacred, because it is ancient. They insist that an age of the world in which God and His angels dwelt afar off in some unthinkable corner of the universe, and the devil and his minions were everywhere near, that such an age only could furnish men competent to formulate a creed worthy of the God of love.

That an age which rejoiced in the burning of witches, the trial and execution of dumb animals as criminals, and the public whipping of church bells for heresy, should give forth the last effort of the race in the expression of true faith in God. Under the guidance of such men the dogmatic traditionalists of to-day are sent as a judgment upon the world. Contrast the attitude of Orthodox assault on science with the spirit of the scientific seekers after truth in this century. Prof. Lincoln of Brown University describes in the "Youth's Companion" a scene which he witnessed at Berlin when he was attending a session of the Royal Academy of Sciences. A large company of learned men had gathered in a handsome academic hall. The members were seated at a long table, at the head of which was the platform occupied by the officers. Prof. Lincoln took a seat near the door, and listened to a paper which one of the learned men was reading. The door was quietly opened while nearly all the members was sitting with their backs to it. A venerable man, with stooping figure and an infirm step, softly crossed the threshold, and seemed anxious to avoid observation. One of the members at the table happened to turn his head, and caught sight of the visitor. Instantly he rose in his place. The president of the academy, glancing across the room, also sprang to his feet. Then one member after another recognized the impressive face and figure of the old man who was quietly making his way toward the seat reserved for him, and before he had reached it the whole company were on their feet. The learned man who was reading the paper was silent, and officers, members and spectators remained standing until the aged visitor had taken a seat. The guest was Alexander Humboldt, then in his eighty-eighth year, infirm in body, but vigorous in mind. The academy paid him a unique tribute of silent reverence as the hoary leader of modern science. There was no applause when he entered the hall, and neither clapping of hands nor shuffling of feet when he took his seat. They stood in their places as though a king had come in among them, and then silently resumed their seats, and listened to the reading of the scientific paper.

Orthodox religion alone can claim the crowning stupidity of heading the assault on Humboldt and his school! These holy simpletons have driven manhood from the modern church. The congregations of your ordinary traditionalism to-day are composed of about four women to one man. The men have formed themselves into scores of secret societies outside of the church. These societies many of them, have more of real Chritianity than the churches they have undermined. A real human brotherhood is their basis; a vital religion is their bond of unity. This is an awful indictment of the dead formalism and ecclesiastical dry rot with which our churches are afflicted. I know of some co-operative societies of workingmen who make no pretentions to religion, who are embodying in life the spirit and teachings of Jesus Christ in a higher degree than scores of churches I know. There are "infidel" clubs in this very city that may go into the kingdom of heaven before some churches.

ALIENATED THE MASSES.

These champions of traditionalism have neglected and alienated the masses of the people, emptied the churches, and produced a collapse of organic church life in the centres of our civilization. Here you touch the secret of our fatal up-town movement of churches. Why do they move up-town? Simply because tradition refuses to readjust itself to a changed civilization. They thus become apostles of the gospel of geography. They say the people have moved up-town—that the people have gone. Take your stand there beside one of those great church buildings being torn down. Do you want people? As far as the eye can reach, rolls a restless ocean of humanity.

These are the men who have in large measures driven spiritual religion out of the church.

Dr. Bruce, of Scotland, well said: "I certainly believe that

there are many more unpolished diamonds hidden in the churchless mass of humanity than the respectable church going part of the community has any idea of. I am even disposed to think that a great and steadily increasing portion of the moral worth of society lies outside of the Church, separated from it, not by godlessness but rather by exceptionally moral earnestness. Many, in fact, have left the church in order to be Christians."
—Kingdom of God, p. 144.

There is being built in fact a vast Church outside the Church. Men have emphasized the tithing of mint and cummin, neglecting the weightier matters of the law, judgment and mercy and faith, until they have destroyed faith in the minds of thousands.

Is it not time we should turn on the light in every department of human thought? Will my creed suffer? If so, let it suffer. If I am wrong, the man who shows where I am wrong is my friend. I shall thank him for it. I rejoice in a free conscience. It is my birthright as a man.

Let the prophets of the race move forward with fearless tread! The church must be rescued from the curse of traditionalism or die. Let us adapt our methods of work to the needs of the hour—to the end that men will be reached and saved.

CHAPTER VII.

The Success of the Salvation Army.

The Salvation Army not only holds its own among the deserted thousands of down-town New York, but builds here its great barracks and lifts its banners triumphant amid the ruins of cowardly churches that have moved up-town.

Why?

Because they use common sense methods of work. They have become all things to all men, if by all means they may save some.

They are the bearers of good news, and their feet are swift. "How beautiful are the feet of them that bring glad tidings!" They are in earnest and they believe they are commissioned to bear a divine message to the world. Children, some time ago, in a vacant lot in Philadelphia, were found playing with bank checks—a valuable bundle of which had been lost from the mail. The little fellows seemed to have an idea that it was commercial paper, and they were playing bank—had established a play bank and were doing a thriving business. They were handling money which had kept the wires hot from city to city trying in vain to find it, and when found of course the messengers hastened to gather up the precious documents and file them away. So it seems to me sometimes the church has been playing with great truths. Our churches have set themselves down in some favored, quiet nooks where people are not likely to disturb them, where the police will not interfere with them or passersby intrude, and there they play at the great work of a world's salvation. There with sacred script, with these messages as good as gold, they play at church, at saving men, at the great work God has commissioned them to do in earnest.

If you look at the work of this army you will find they are

dead in earnest. They know the value of the script they handle, and they go on swift feet to carry it to those who need it most.

They do not build churches, they build men. The early apostolic church did not build church buildings; they had no time. It was not until Christianity began to crystallize and to fossilize in the forms of institutions that men began to build tombs in which to place it. These men who have thus sought to revive apostolic Christianity have gone in the same ways as the first disciple of Jesus Christ went forth into the world, using all institutions that exist, if by all these means they may reach and save men—"all things to all men if by all means some may be saved." In India they become Indians; in America, Americans. In the wilds of a savage nation they would go and adopt their customs and dress, if need be, to save them. What a contrast to our institutional Christianity!

WITHIN THE SHADOW OF ST. MARK'S.

John Ruskin describes in marvelous language the great Cathedral of St. Mark. It is as though some wonderful artist had taken the brush of genius and painted before your very eyes its glory. And, after he finishes that wonderful description, he turns his attention to the people that surge before the cathedral doors and says that not one of them—not a passerby, not a soldier or civilian, not a beggar or huckster, not a solitary soul of the great crowd—ever looks up at its beauty.

But up against the very foundation stones the huckster pushes his stall. Within its shadow the soldiers discourse their music, which drowns the sound of the great organ. And, without, lounging like lizards basking in the sun, are the men who, with their stiletto, would stab in the heart every musician that pipes to them, did they dare. And the images of Christ and the saints look down on it all! Oh, paraphrase of ancient Jerusalem, where in her temples they bought and sold! Institutions, glorious in form, ceremonies magnificent—but a lapse and lost mass of people surge by your cathedral and your temple, unmindful of its

THE SUCCESS OF THE SALVATION ARMY.   71

existence, with the devil in their heart, and with all the powers of destruction growing in every muscle and transmitted generation unto generation, piling wrath against wrath, against that day, when up to the doors of that cathedral will surge a mob that will raze it to the ground and leave not one stone upon another unless he who ministers at the altar within shall remember that Jesus Christ came not to build institutions, but to save men.

NOT CHURCH POLITICIANS.

In their purpose and methods they are also Christlike. They are the friends of the poor and outcast world, and so was Jesus Christ. Not where they can get the most do they locate their stations, but where they can do the most. When we build our churches we want the best plot in the city, where the grand boulevard intersects the great cross-town street, where the elite are moving, where the bankers and brokers are congregating—there buy a lot and build your church, and you will rent your pews at the highest possible rate.

In the results of their work they show the world that they are true disciples of Christ. Do they represent the true spirit of the true Christ? Come before them and ask the same supreme test John asked of Christ, and take the answer Jesus gave and apply it to them.

John sent to Jesus and asked Him if He be the Messiah, or if another should be expected,, and Jesus replied telling him the lame walk, the blind see, the deaf hear, the dead are raised, and, climax of all, the poor have the Gospel preached to them. Stand before the church to-day and submit to it this supreme test. Stand before the army of cranks to-day and submit to them this supreme test and hear the answer. You say: "What is all this noise with which you have come to disturb the peace and civilization of the twentieth century? Are you disciples of Jesus?" They can answer you in the words of Jesus Christ, "Go and tell the questioners that the lame walk, the blind see, the lepers are cleansed; that the dead are raised and the poor have the Gospel preached to them."

THAT ONE MAN BOOTH.

The Bishop of Winchester says: "If ever the masses are to be converted it must be by an organized lay body. The Salvation Army has set the church the example of courage." Canon Liddon, whose voice thrilled the world, after attending a Salvation Army meeting with Mr. Stead, said: "It filled me with shame. I feel guilty when I think of myself. To think of these poor people, with their imperfect grasp of truth—what a contrast between what they and we are doing! When I see how little we produce, compared with what that meeting exhibited, I take shame to myself."

John Morley, "free thinker," skeptic, said in 1880: "We have all been on the wrong track, and the result is less to show than that one man Booth. Oh, we children of light—Spencer, Arnold, Harrison and the rest—spend our lives in endeavoring to dispel superstition and bring in an era based on reason, education and enlightened self-interest, but this man has produced more direct effect upon this generation than all of us put together." Mr. Stead says: "The Army has deserved well of the State because, training the people in self-government, it has done more to spread the genuine culture among the masses than Cambridge and Oxford."

It is needless to multiply those testimonies from great men. They are convincing. The voice of the Christian world, the voice of the independent thinking world to-day, is practically a unit as to the results of the work of this Army.

STONED AND CURSED.

Yet they were mobbed and stoned and cursed. So were Jesus and His Disciples, and any movement, that starts in this world and is not cursed and stoned and mobbed, you may be certain of one thing—that there is too close a connection between that movement and the world itself, for if a man attempts to really reach and save this world, he must go along the lines not on which the world itself moves, but he must take the model, Jesus Christ, and if he does he will land on Calvary, if he lives that life to its inevitable, logical conclusion. This is the first sign of genuine discipleship of Jesus Christ. They were stoned and cursed and hissed by the world and the church.

They were accused of sensationalism, and all the sins that come from it, especially by the church. Being sensational they were strictly apostolic and Christlike. The apostle Paul was a great sensationalist—that is, he was fool enough to say: "I will be all things to all men, if by that means I may save some. When I go to Athens I will be an Athenian, and I will go where they are." And he went and stirred things up wherever he went. When he went into a town they were sometimes so excited that they dragged him before the magistrate and put him out. The men who followed Jesus were thus sensational. They had to be if they preached Christ.

SACRED RHEUMATISM.

For Christ himself was a sensation. From the day as a little child he sent back that sensational message to His mother in the Temple, "I am about my father's business," to the day He attacked Scribe and Pharisee and said: "You miserable hypocrites, whited sepulchers, full of dead men's bones within, beautiful without, you make long prayers; you stand in public places, and your hearts are black as hell. O generation of vipers, who hath warned you to flee from the wrath to come?" To whom is He talking? To the priests and bishops and cardinals—the great churchmen of His day. He was talking about the established church to the men who sat in the seat of Moses and delivered the law to the people—the men unto whom had been delivered the statutes of the most high God. From the day He began to work His miracles at Cana of Galilee, down to the end, He was a sensationalist in the highest and truest sense of the word, and anybody that really does the work of Christ is bound to stir things wherever he goes, and if he does not he has failed to touch the true heart and life of the Christ.

For my own part I would rather be a drummer in the Salvation Army and bang an old drum through this world for the salvation of men than stand in the mightiest cathedral on this earth and preach the most glorious Gospel to a handful of good old men and women who are so old in the faith that they have sacred rheumatism. I had rather be a human sandwich and march through the streets with the Gospel written on my back and breast, and preach the Gospel thus, than stand beneath Gothic arches in your most magnificent frescoed church and spout to vacant pews. I would rather be an old John Pounds, of Portsmouth, with a hot potato in my hand—he took one and stuck it under the nose of boys in the streets, until he saved 500 and made them magnificent men—I would rather wield that hot potato for the salvation of men than wear the tiara of Leo XIII. and sit on the throne of St. Peter's before the assembled pilgrims of the world.

Is there a man so dull in the world to-day that does not know that William Booth and his sainted wife were God's own prophets. Not one! Yet remember the reception which they first met.

There are some lessons the church ought to get from this army. First, in the Salvation Army it does not take a long creed to save the world. Look at our creed tinkers to-day, with their hammers and nails and old manuscripts, tinkering away at the creeds of the world. I thank God for the example of men, fool enough to believe that all that is necessary for a creed is to believe in the Father, His Son, Jesus, and to love the man that He came and died for so tenderly and deeply that he is willing to go down into the ditch and put his arms under him and say to him in his rags and filth, "My brother, I love you."

The only creed needed in this world to save it to-day is the vital creed Jesus Christ preached, "Thou shalt love the Lord thy God with all thy heart, thy neighbor as thyself." And that is all the creed of the Salvation Army. What a lesson to the church to-day raking up the ashes of the dead past and trying to fan the embers to a flame, that from it they may light again martyr fires!

The church should understand too, from the army's methods, that the way to reach the masses is to go for them. What is the matter with our churches? They are afraid of disturbing their ancestors. I read an editorial the other day about a railroad built in Jerusalem and of the mourning over the desecration of the Holy Land by the engine. You would have thought the Emperor of China wrote it. They have kept the steam engine out of China for centuries because it would disturb the supposed sanctity of the soil. As though those old hills in Palestine were God's temple only! Jesus said, "Neither at Jerusalem or these mountains is to be the place where God shall dwell, but he is to dwell in the hearts of men." You might run a steam engine all over Palestine, plant it all in foreign fruits and desecrate every spot there and Christianity will be just as glorious.

FROM DITCH AND GUTTER.

If the church does not do the work of saving the world God will raise up a church from the ditch and gutter—that has nothing to do with the established church—that will do the work He came into the world to do. Some of our good brethren met the other day in congress and discussed the question whether a certain ritual should read, "He descended into hell" or "went down into hell." Think of bringing the scholarship of the world to bear on a question like that while the world outside is literally tumbling into hell! Whether they "descend" or "go down into"—they get there!

A lady once sat at a table beside a distinguished scientist, supposed to be Prof. Huxley, and asked him if it was not a serious thing that the vicar should turn his face to the East in administering the sacrament. He said: "My dear madam, Sir John

Herschel says that if there were a limitless sea between this planet and the nearest big star, and in sailing over it you should drop a pea at the end of every mile, it would take 10,000 ships of 600 tons burden each, each loaded to the water line with peas, to reach that star. Do you suppose that He who made such a universe really minds whether the vicar turns his face to the East or West, North or South?"

The Phillippine Islanders are a people who venerate sleep. They think it sacrilegious for a man to disturb another while he sleeps, especially if he steps over his sleeping body. I know churches that venerate the idea of sleeping, and if another man should step over them while they slept they would go into sacred spasms! And yet we think we are civilized and smile at those poor inhabitants of savage islands.

The one serious hindrance to the future expansion of the Army is the Imperialism of Gen. Booth. There are signs of the end now appearing. This future is thoroughly unchristian and will be modified or the Army will cease to be a power.

CHAPTER VIII.

The Apparent Success of the Episcopal Church.

Apparently the only exception to the universal failure of Protestantism in New York is to be found in the Episcopal Church. While other branches of Protestantism have failed to hold the c...dren born into their homes during the past decade, from the year 1885 to 1892, the Episcopal Church increased its membership from 30,000 to 39,000, in round numbers. That is to say, their net gain was about 9,000. This is a little more than the normal birth-rate of the membership, and while it is no great success, it stands as an oasis in the desert that calls for a particular examination as to the causes. The causes, as set forth by an enthusiastic exponent of the church, in criticism of my statements, are as follows:

RITUALISM.

"That solemn, beautiful, dignified, sacred worship of God which is embodied in the ritual of the ancient church is denied to the devotees of Protestantism, hence men go to secret societies, where they find at least an imitation of it. Again, the preaching function has been exalted to such a degree that the worship of God (apart from the sermon), which old-fashioned Christians regarded as the most important and sacred part of the service, is now commonly called 'preliminary exercises!' Worship is made a mere side issue, and to hear a man talk is regarded as the motive for going to church. That being so, how can we expect a lawyer, who very often can make a more stirring speech in behalf of a ragged pickpocket than some preachers can in behalf of religion, or a drummer who extols his brand of soap with more eloquence than the average minister his doc-

78 APPARENT SUCCESS OF THE EPISCOPAL CHURCH.

trine, how can we expect such men to go to church for the sake of sermons? Return to their places the divine liturgy, the solemn worship of God, and above all the Holy Sacraments which operate on the soul not by man power, or rhetoric, or hero-worship, but by the action of the Holy Spirit. Give back to men the supernatural elements of Christianity that Protestantism has robbed them of, and they will go to church. In the words of an eminent Scotch Presbyterian divine: 'Our pepole have been estranged through the weariness of preaching. Down with the pulpit and up with the Mass.'"

PHILLIPS BROOKS

In answer to this criticism I would simply say, I do not believe that the ritual of the Episcopal Church in America, is a help; but I believe, upon the other hand, that it is in some ways a hindrance to the advancement of their cause. Canon Barrett of London, says, in so many words, that the ritual of the church is an impediment in the efforts to reach the masses of the people; that the direct services, direct prayer and direct speech of the other denominations are more powerful weapons in reaching and holding the working people of England. The Episcopal Church was first in the field in America, controlled the legislatures, and controlled society, in a majority of the Colonies. It has failed to hold those States, and to-day occupies one of the subordinate positions, in point of membership, in the Protestant ranks in America, numbering, all told, about 500,000 adherents, in a total of 13,000,000. The ritual has been a positive hindrance in the way of the spread of the church and its work. What they have done they have done in spite of this, not because of it. Besides, my reverend critic evidently belongs to the school of the High Church, and this faction of the Episcopal faith has done little to build up the church, in my judgment, but has been a constant feeder of Roman Catholicism. The motto with which he closes —"Down with the pulpit and up with the Mass"—shows the tendency of his mind. The Episcopal Church in this country has been powerful as its pulpit has been a power. One of the most powerful preachers that America has produced was Phillips Brooks. Does my reverend critic mean to say that he could increase the power of the Episcopal Church by destroying the pulpit of such men as Brooks and hoisting the Mass instead? This is sacred nonsense.

It seems to me that the reasons for the apparent success of the Episcopal Church in New York City are peculiarly local, and do not apply to the Church throughout the United States. It seems to me that there are three reasons for this success.

THE POWER OF MONEY.

First, is the enormous money power concentrated within this church in the city of New York. It is said that Trinity corporation alone has invested property worth $150,000,000. The entire valuation of all the property of other Protestant denominations in the city of New York does not reach $17,000,000. There are several Episcopal churches in the city whose annual budget of expenditures exceeds $50,000. This is a tremendous power. It has been possible with these enormous resources for the Episcopal Church to go into new neighborhoods, buy a whole block, erect a palatial church without a member, build a magnificent school-house and parish-house, place a full organization of teachers and clergymen in charge, and in two years have a flourishing establishment.

It seems to me, a second reason why this church has specially succeeded in New York is that its churches are well manned. While other Protestant denominations have adhered to the idea of a one man ministry, the Episcopal Church has placed three, four, five men, in charge of each parish. From the exceedingly astute and scholarly Bishop, who presides over the diocese, down through its various ranks, their churches are superbly officered. They have recognized the fact that one man cannot do the work of ten.

Third, I believe they have succeeded because the church has recognized more fully and fairly the social aspects of Christianity. They have recognized the breadth of the Christianity of Christ in its application to the whole life of man, and here have placed themselves in touch with the spirit of the new life of the century. This cannot be said of the Episcopal Church generally in the United States. It is true in Boston, it is true in New York. I do not know another great city of which so much can be said. Certainly no such statement applies to the church from the point of view of the nation. If you ask the question, is the Church of England, of which the Church of America is but a branch—if you ask the question, in other words, if the Episcopal Church is advancing or decaying, I would answer by quoting the words of Dr. Momerie, the representative of the Church of England at the World's Congress of Religions. Hear what he says upon the

"DECADENCE OF THE ENGLISH CHURCH."

"There is much in my church which I admire and love. Its music, its architecture, many of its prayers, a few of its hymns, a little of its teachings, much of its practice, some of its associations, connected as they have been with the great joys and sorrows of life, the unselfish devotion of a large number of its clergy, these things are of inestimable value. But I am convinced that the good is being neutralized by the evil, and that there is a danger of both speedily perishing in one common catastrophe. The church is in imminent peril—all the more imminent because it is seldom recognized or suspected. In one of his humorous poems, Oliver Wendell Holmes speaks of an old couple who had been accustomed for many years to drive about in a 'one-horse shay.' This carriage was constructed originally on an ingenious principal, so that every part should be just as strong as every other part. It was a sort of infallible chaise: there was not a weak point about it; it never seemed any the worse for wear; it looked as if it would last forever. But on one occasion, as it was being driven along in the usual fashion, it suddenly collapsed—into dust. I am afraid that may be an emblem of what is in store for the Church of England. To superficial observers she appears prosperous and flourishing; but nevertheless the end may be near. and the end is near, unless the clergy can be awakened to a sense of the danger before it is too late.

"Institutions, like organisms, must—if they would survive—adapt themselves to their environment. Want of adaptation is death. Human society is constantly changing, in its modes of thought, in its experiences, in its needs. And unless the church changes correspondingly she will be destroyed—destroyed by the very society which she claims to mould. But the clergy, with few exceptions, persistently refuses to recognize this necessity for adaptation. The modern priest, as a rule, expects as much credulity on the part of his devotees as did the old medicine-men and rain-makers. He talks about miracles—Gadarene pigs and what not—as he might have done at a time when natural law had never been heard of; when every one believed, not in the uniformity, but in the irregularity of nature. He talks about inspiration and revelation as if he did not know that much of the teaching of the Bible had been equalled, and even surpassed, in other sacred literatures, and that some of the sayings of Christ Himself—including even the golden rule—had been anticipated by 'pagans' hundreds of years before the Christian era. The dogmas of orthodoxy were formulated in the third or fourth century, and yet he goes on repeating these antiquated shibboleths as if he were not aware that since the days of St. Augustine men's views of the universe, and, therefore, of the God of the universe, had been revolutionized. Change and progress are hateful to the clerical mind. Instead of aiding development, the clergy have eternally hampered and opposed it. Instead of leading the race, it has been their mournful prerogative to lag behind. The majority of them are now centuries in the rear. And the consequence is that men are beginning to ask themselves if they might not dispense with the 'benefit of clergy,' if they would not be better off without a church than with it?

A DECLINING MINISTRY.

"The influence of the priesthood is everywhere on the wane. Fashion, no doubt, continues to lend it a certain precarious support.

'At church on Sunday to attend
Will serve to keep the world your friend.'

But going to church is no longer absolutely indispensable. The friendship of the world may be obtained without it. Even the 'smart' people are becoming lax in their religious observances. I remember a few years ago it was proposed in convocation to pass a resolution condemning 'the desecration of the Sabbath,' which was then becoming so common in society. But the Bishop of London, with touching frankness, said that they might as well save themselves the trouble, as nobody would pay attention to the resolution if they did pass it. And over the cultured portion of the community the influence of the Church is already almost nil. How many clever persons do you know who are in the habit of looking to their clergymen for instruction? Even the scholarly clergy—those who are thoroughly acquainted with Hebrew and with the Fathers—even they, with few exceptions, are quite out of touch with modern thought. And every year their ranks are recruited from a lower intellectual class, so that the small amount of influence which the clergy still retain is continually becoming smaller.

"For the last thirty or forty years the intellectual attainments of candidates for Orders have been steadily on the decline. The Church is ceasing to attract young men of conspicuous ability. At the English universities in the olden times the best men usually went into Orders; but what was formerly the rule is now the exception. This is a fact which it is idle to attempt to dis-

APPARENT SUCCESS OF THE EPISCOPAL CHURCH. 83

pute. Every student at Oxford and Cambridge is acquainted with it. It can be proved to demonstration by comparing the ordination lists of to-day with those of half a century ago. It has been acknowledged and deplored by the Bishops themselves. In 1861, Dr. Temple, then head-master of Rugby, wrote a remarkable letter to Dr. Tait, who was at that time Bishop of London. This letter was called forth by the fact that Dr. Temple, in common with other contributors to the 'Essays and Reviews,' had been severely censured by the Bishops in convocation. 'Many years ago,' he said, 'your lordship urged us from the university pulpit to undertake the critical study of the Bible. You said it was a dangerous study, but indispensable. You described its difficulties, and those who listened to you must have felt a confidence that, if they took your advice, you at any rate would never join in treating them unjustly if their study had brought with it the difficulties you described. To tell a man to study, and yet bid him under heavy penalties come to the same conclusions as those who have not studied, is to mock him. If the conclusions are prescribed the study is precluded. Freedom plainly implies the widest possible toleration. I admit that toleration must have limits, or the church would fall to pieces. But the student has a right to claim, first, that those limits should be known beforehand and contained in formularies within his own reach, not locked up in the breasts of certain of his brethren; secondly, that his having transgressed them should be decided after fair, open trial by men practised in such decisions. Instead of that what do we see? A set of men publish a book containing the results of their study and thought, which—rightly or wrongly—they believe to be within the limits traced out by the formularies. Suddenly, without any warning that they are on their trail, without any opportunity given for explanation or defense, assuredly without any proof that they have really transgressed the limits prescribed, the whole Bench of Bishops join in inflicting a severe censure and in insinuating that they are dishonest men. How on earth is any study to be pursued under such treatment as this? You complain that young men of ability will not take Orders. How can you expect it when this is what befalls any one who does not think as you do.'

MR. GLADSTONE.

"The fact that the ablest men have ceased to go into Orders received a curious kind of indirect confirmation in a speech made by Mr. Gladstone at the Jubilee of Trinity College, Glenalmond, in October, 1891. 'The charge that the clergy are falling behind in the intellectual race,' he said, 'I believe to be a most inaccurate, most untrue, and most unjust aspersion. You may judge of the character of a body in part by the names of those who die in its ranks. I will name five men who have died in the ranks of the British clergy within the last two years. One of these was Bishop Lightfoot, and one Dr. Liddon; one was Dean Church; one was Archbishop Magee; and the fifth, a much younger man, whose fame was almost entirely confined to the University of Oxford, Mr. Aubrey Moore. Now I say that body is an illustrious body from whose ranks, within less than two years, five such men can be numbered as having ceased to be.' True. But to know whether that body is or is not degenerating, we must inquire by whom the dead are to be succeeded. The fact that the English army was once led by a Marlborough and a Wellington would not ensure for it victory to-day. And since young men of ability are no longer taking Orders, it follows that eventually there will be no worthy successors of the eminent clergymen who have gone.

"All the while laymen are being better educated; they are reading more widely and thinking more deeply. They are going up-hill as fast as the clergy are going down. The intellectual advances of the laity render the clergy less and less capable of understanding them, so that the want of adaptation between society and the church is ever on the increase; and want of adaptation is death. There is no possibility of evading this law. Ridicule will not alter it; it is not to be laughed out of existence.

APPARENT SUCCESS OF THE EPISCOPAL CHURCH.

Reasoning will not change it; it is not to be argued away. For a while, no doubt, it may be ignored; it may seemingly be disobeyed with impunity; but the effects of the disobedience are only accumulating for a more terrible catastrophe in the end. Unless the Church of England undergoes a radical change, she will practically cease to exist. She will appeal exclusively to the intellectual dregs of the community, and could only therefore in bitterest irony be called a National Church."

CHAPTER IX.

The Strength of Roman Catholicism.

Does Roman Catholicism hold to-day any possible solution for the failure of Protestantism in New York? The faithful priest of Rome will answer as a matter of course in the affirmative.

For my own part I gladly grant to the Roman Catholic Church the full measure of praise due for their good work in New York. I rejoice in much they have done. Before we look at the painful facts let us present the bright ones.

In the Roman Catholic Church there has been a degree of progress, a revolutionary change of front, within the past few years, which has been nothing short of a miracle. We are profoundly interested in their affairs, Protestants though we are.

We are interested because they represent the majority of the Christian world, numbering Christian nations numerically. The Roman Catholics embrace something like 200,000,000 of the inhabitants of Christendom, and whatever their errors in the past have been they are our brethren in Christ. Whatever may be the gulf that separates us to-day from them, the development of Christianity in the future will have no history that will not have as part of its fundamental development the story of this great power, which we have called the Roman Catholic Church. It has stood the assault of centuries—the assaults of men within the church and without.

In forming an estimate of other religions we need to be careful. All religions have in them elements of the divine. Whether it is the religion of the savage that bows down before a miserable image in the heart of the wilds of an unexplored forest, whether the Chinaman before his idol in China, or the Japanese in Japan—wherever you find man looking up with inquiring heart after God—you are walking on holy ground, and there will

THE STRENGTH OF ROMAN CATHOLICISM.

be found imbedded in that religion a something that you must respect—something of the divine. It is a fact that most of us have our denominational differences to-day because of our education. I am a Baptist because my father was. You are a Methodist because your father was. If my father had been a Roman Catholic, I have not the slightest doubt I would be a Catholic to-day.

THE CATHOLICS IN AMERICA.

We are interested and tremendously so in the development of Catholicism in America because America holds in one sense the key to history. Mr. Gladstone, while he represents the high mark of English liberalism, while he is an intense Englishman in everything, says that the next century is to place the crown of empire of the world on the brow of America, and he figures out that you are to have on this continent 365,000,000 of inhabitants at the close of the century now about to dawn upon us. Whatever we may do at present about emigration, we are destined to receive from all nations of the earth a continued stream of life, seeking a wider and freer outlook.

Is the Catholic Church in America to be an enemy to be crushed, or can it be made an ally in the work of saving the world?

In forming conditions of judgment on a question like this you must take the sum total of their influence. Bob Burdette gives an illustration of the wrong tendency in this direction when he commented the other day on a Unitarian's report of the religious condition of Japan. The Unitarian said that when he asked a Japanese what he thought of the converts of evangelical churches in that section of heathendom he replied "with a meaning smile," Burdette says, "That is information from headquarters." If you want to find out about Christian converts go to the heathen for information. If you want to find out about the Democratic party ask the Republican. If you want to find out about the Methodists go to the Baptists. If you want to find out the facts about a man straight from the very fountain head, always go to the enemy of the man about whom you want your information, and you are certain to get it. It would not be fair if we consulted only those sources of information about Catholicism.

Fox's book of Martyr's has doubtless served its purpose in freeing the human conscience from the tyranny of Rome. But the mild insanity that identifies the scarlet woman of the Apocalypse with the Pope of Rome surely has no serious mission to perform in the nineteenth century.

THE NEW CENSUS.

The census of 1890 records the names of 380,000 adherents of the Roman Catholic Church in New York. The Christian world should rejoice in this measure of success in any church in a city whose dominant spirit is hostile to all religion.

Nine-tenths of our doctrinal principles are identical with the Catholics; the one-tenth on which we differ is the question of ecclesiastical machinery. And Rome herself is coming to democracy, and when she agrees to the great fundamental principles of a democratic government in the State she will come at last to the other, for the State yields the basis on which the church will be built in the future.

The Church of Rome in this city is doing a work for the foreign masses we are not doing. This town could not be held from the devil for twenty-four hours if it were not for the power of the Catholic priesthood. You would have to turn your guns into these streets and sweep them with grape and canister without them. What have we done to reach these people? Nothing. What are we going to do? Nothing. Who are doing that work? The Jewish rabbis and the Catholic priests. If they do not do it, it is not done. If you take those forces away, you have left the people absolutely in darkness. If that is a fact, we must recognize it, and that these forces are being utilized for good.

I admire the wisdom and skill of the Catholic priesthood. They have more common sense than Protestant ministers. They are more skillful. They have longer heads. They know better how to grasp and hold a city. Go and look at their big churches here to-day. In my Western trips the biggest churches I see are the Catholic churches. They were the first in the town, before the other denominations thought of building, and the priests got the lots for nothing, too—long-headed men that look far into the future and seize their opportunities and hold on to them forever. While other churches lost their rights to title in this city, they had the sense to go to the Legislature and have their titles perfected, while we were asleep. They do not preach on Sunday and say to the people, "You can go to the devil during the week." They teach their people that what they preach on Sunday is to be put into life on Monday, and the priest can say things that have great power and influence in the political world. If Senator David B. Hill said, "Give me the saloons, and you can have the churches," he was talking about the Protestant churches, not the Catholic. Why? Because our Protestant churches are a disorganized mob.

CHRISTIAN IS AS CHRISTIAN DOES.

From Catholicism to-day we should learn the concrete application of truth in everyday life. The question is, in fact, what a Christian does, not what he professes. We have the best creed —the creed in the abstract—but Christian is what Christian does. I have been alarmed about some things in the Protestant world as I watched the progress of Rome. The Pope of Rome has showed, in this age, that he knows the drift of the century; that he has adjusted the whole machinery of Rome to that drift, and that he has felt the pulse of the social age; that the masses are going to rule the world, and he is going to be the friend of the masses, and rule them. If you are going to keep up with Rome, you must know those facts as thoroughly as the Pope knows them to-day. We have the creed, but be careful that you put it into practice. Practice is what tells in the Christian world, not paper creeds or theory.

Catholics are liberal givers. When Dr. McGlynn was turned

out of St. Stephen's Church, the collection amounted to $2,500 on a single Sunday. There are no rich people in that parish— all poor people, but they are taught to give; it is part of their religion and life. If a Catholic dies, he remembers the church. A Presbyterian died the other day in New York. He was worth nearly a hundred millions. But the will he left was simply this: "Lord have mercy on me and my wife, my son John and his wife, we four and no more! Amen."

Inside of every Protestant denomination there are powers of wealth concentrated that if they were only poured into the church, as Rome has her wealth poured into her bosom, what a power we might be for good! Miss Drexel could give her $8,000,000 in a single gift to educate the negroes and Indians, and we have only one or two men in our Protestant world that seem alive to the importance of the salvation of a world.

Who runs the hospitals in this city to-day? The Catholics. We have a few other hospitals, but they do not sum up in the total. We have been mighty on creeds, but broken down when we came into life. Mighty are we in exploring the doctrine of Pauline faith, but when we came to the parable of the Good Samaritan we turned that over to the Catholics, whom we look down on with suspicion.

I thank God to-day for the indications in the Catholic world of such progress as we see. I hail it with rejoicing, as one who loves Jesus. When He shall reign supreme He will bring many Catholics and many Protestants together. When that time comes, errors that now are strong will be eliminated in the process of development, and God will bring one out of many.

CHAPTER X.
The Decay of Romanism.

The system of Romanism can hold no solution of the religious problem of our centres of life in America, for a very simple reason. Its decay has been in many respects more serious than the failure of Protestantism.

Max Muller has declared, as the result of a life-study of all religions: "The one universal characteristic of all religions is decay." This is the incontrovertible testimony of history. That is to say, forms die, creeds pass, rites and systems change, yet religion remains the one eternal fact of humanity. If the Apostles should return to earth to-day and enter those churches that make the loudest boasts of being "Apostolic," they would not know how to behave. They would be lost in wonder at the elaborate ritual of the great Roman Catholic and Apostolic Church. The Apostle Peter would be utterly at sea if he should attempt to join in a high mass at St. Peter's, Rome.

Religion expresses itself in terms of the knowledge of the age. The evolution of religion is a simple historic fact. In no two countries of the human race does the religion which bears the same name mean the same thing. This is so, simply because the knowledge of the race grows with each succeeding generation, and the expression of religion must adjust itself to this increase of knowledge, or perish in the resulting conflict.

IMPERIALISM.

Now Romanism cannot possibly hold any solution of the religious problem of modern New York, because the system is essentially ancient. The essence of Romanism is the principle of imperialism. This principle was finally crystallized into the dogma of Papal Infallibility in 1870. Such a dogma was inevitable and strictly logical. Imperialism is the soil of the Roman system. It always has been, it always will be. When Romanism ceases to be imperialism, it ceases to be Romanism. The present Pope of Rome recently made overtures to the English Church for "Christian Union." When an official of the Church of England asked Cardinal Vaughan, the Pope's representative in England, what must be the basis of this proposed union, the Cardinal promptly replied: "Submission to the supremacy of the Pope." No other answer could have been given without Romanism stultifying the reason for its existence.

The growth and the decay of the principle of Imperialism is the one great fact that fills the volume of the history of man during the 3,000 years of our historic record. No one doubts that the development of the empire of the imperial ruler above the petty tribal kings and tyrants was a vast gain for the human race. Imperialism had its part to play in the evolution of the civilization of man. But the climax of the drama of empire is in the past. We are now rapidly approaching the day of the triumph of Democracy. Empires are the dung-heaps now out of which republics grow.

ROME'S CLIMAX.

The system of Romanism reached its highest development under Pope Innocent III., in the thirteenth century. It held its triumphant splendor for a hundred years. And then began the decay that has been steady and inexorable down to the present hour. This period of imperial splendor is followed by the great scandal of the three Popes, each claiming at the same time to be the only vice-gerent of God on earth, each denouncing the other as impostors and veritable sons of hell! This disgrace involved an immediate loss of prestige and power to the Papacy, from which it did not recover and never has recovered. The kings and princes of Europe made haste to build the defences to their thrones higher and stronger, and were ever afterward able to practically dictate their own terms to the wearer of the tiara. From this period dates the beginning of the emancipation of the "temporal" from the "spiritual" power. And here begins the story of heresy and rebellion within the fold. In the foreground of this strange scene towers the colossal figure of John Wycliffe. They dug up his very bones and burned them for heresy, and scattered the ashes in the waters of a brook, that they might have no resting-place on the earth. The brook carried them to the sea, and the sea carried them round the world, and circled the earth with the spirit of the dead martyr!

The next blow which befell the imperialism of Rome was the pragmatic sanction in France which guaranteed the French Church a practical independence of the central power. It was the beginning of Gallican liberties that has never since been abridged.

Then followed the statutes of Provisors, of Premunire and of Mortmain, by which death-bed bequests and many other rich sources of Roman revenue were curtailed or abolished in England. These laws brought great financial and political damage to the Papacy.

DEATH-CRY OF A GIANT.

All this was to be followed by the thunder-peal of the Reformation of the sixteenth century, under the leadership of Martin Luther. One-half of Europe joined this great rebellion, and when, under the leadership of the reactionist enthusiasts of Loyola, Rome had recovered Bavaria, Bohemia, Hungary and Belgium, the storm of the French Revolution burst with resistless fury. Her priests were butchered, her property confiscated or destroyed, her proud dignitaries hurled to the dust, and the very chair of the Pope, for a time, shattered into splinters. After this storm had passed, and before the damages could be repaired, the Italian rebellions began to drench Italy in blood. One by one the fair provinces of the Papal power were wrested from the Vatican, until at last Victor Emmanuel stood before the walls of Rome with united Italy at his back! As his victorious army sprung over the falling walls of the Empire of the Popes, they were followed by missionaries, distributing cart-loads of Protestant Bibles to the populace of Rome. There are to-day 25,000 members of Protestant Churches in Italy, and there are eleven of their churches in Rome itself, beneath the very shadow of St. Peter's. The dogma of Papal infallibility was promulgated upon the fall of Rome. Of course. It was natural. It was the death-cry of a giant. It meant the embalming of a principle that had fought its life out and died in the last ditch.

The cause of this decay is not far to seek. The decline of the power of Papal Imperialism has been coincident with the growth of the principle of nationality. As England grew into conscious power as a nation and a national spirit began to incarnate itself in her citizenship the King of England was substituted for the Pope of Rome. The growth of the French nation and the consciousness of the part it was to play as a nation in human history forced from the Pope the concession of the rights of the Gallican Church. The growth of the spirit of nationality made the German people with their temperament the inevitable scene of the Reformation's Prologue. Rome lost Italy, the seat of her August Empire of the centuries, because the principle of Imperialism collided with the development of the spirit of Italian Nationality.

AMERICA A BOTTOMLESS WHIRLPOOL.

Likewise, in America, Romanism collided with the spirit of American nationality. The United States of America is the bottomless whirlpool in which millions of Roman Catholics have poured during the last generation, never to appear again! When they have reappeared it was through the baptism unto the new life of the most vigorous nationalism in the history of the world. Henceforth they are Americans! They are as dead to the principle of Roman Imperialism. Since 1820 we have received about 17,000,000 immigrants. More than 10,000,000 of these were Roman Catholics, and yet with seventy years of growth and most prolific birth-rate of any of our classes of people, at the end of this period Romanism can only muster about 7,000,000 nominal adherents, counting population, men, women and children.

Countin the children born of Roman Catholic parentage, the Catholics have lost at least 6,000,000 of their own members within the past two generations. It is no answer to say that the church has grown from a few hundred thousands to millions in this time. The point is, the Catholic population of this nation in 1890, by the Federal census, was only about 6,000,000. It ought to have been 12,000,000 if they could only have held their own people.

THEIR DECAY IN NEW YORK.

Take the city of New York and test the question. The foreign population of New York—that is, foreign-born and the children of the foreign-born, is eighty per cent. of the total. The Catholic population of the city by the census of 1890 is 380,000—twenty per cent.! By a careful examination of the sources of our immigration it will be found that at least fifty-four per cent. of it is Roman Catholic. This should give the Roman Catholic Church an aggregate of 972,000 in New York City. It actually is only 380,000, showing a loss in New York alone of 592,000! Protestantism has not held its own in New York. The record of Roman Catholicism is even worse.

Imperialism coming in conflict with the spirit of freedom goes down before it. Imperialism commands obedience. Freedom invites reason. When the pent-up manhood of the Old World Imperial traditionalism catches the spirit of American nationality it is lost forever to the Roman system. The conflict with democracy is a conflict with the conquering power of the ages. The claim of an extraneous mechanical "Authority" from on high has been the secret of every tyranny that has ever oppressed man. Men have begun to see this clearly at last. The tyrants who ruled Egypt claimed divine authority to rule wrongly. So the rulers of ancient India; so did the Caesars; so did the Bourbons in France. This day is happily past in the history of the advanced nations of the world. The survival of the Imperialism of Rome, even in its attenuated form is an anachronism. The rights of office everywhere yield to the rights of man. Triumphant Demos conquers the world, and the empire is but the prelude to the republic.

Another potent cause of the decay of Romanism in America is the loss of control over child life, incident to the establishment and maintenance of the public schools.

CHILDHOOD AND RELIGION.

Childhood is the hour of religious training. It is the real basis of all the differences of sect and cult. Our religious bias is created for us in the growth of the fibre of the child mind. Even when reason has developed its powers, these very powers will be prostituted to the defense of, rather than used for, the destruction of that bias. Some negroes taught my little boy to believe in ghosts. I tried to clear his mind of this superstition when he grew a little older. He would have none of my explanations. I told him it was utterly absurd; that there was no such thing as a ghost. In reply he asked me in the utmost amazement: "What! Don't you believe any ghosts?" I told him emphatically not.

"What!" he exclaimed with deep seriousness, "Not even in the Holy Ghost?"

Is it any wonder that a distinguished Roman Catholic bishop should say, "Give me the mind of a child until he is seven years old and you can have him the rest of his life." This is peculiarly the strength and the weakness of the Roman system. The sacerdotal conception of marriage, so strongly insisted upon, is based upon the absolute necessity of controlling the offspring of the union. The institution of civic marriage was a blow at the very heart of the whole scheme of Roman Imperialism.

THE PUBLIC SCHOOLS.

The energy of the Roman hierarchy in America has been given to the school problem of necessity. As the adult population from the Catholic countries of the Old World has reached America, it has melted by millions into the stream of American national life and spirit before their very eyes. And the priesthood has been utterly powerless to prevent this. The only possible remedy lay in the training of the child-mind in the ideals of Imperialism as they grew in power in the native air of the freedom of the republic. Hence the gigantic effort in their poverty to build a complete system of parochial school that should cripple, at least, the influence and power of the schools of the republic. This effort has been only partially successful. It is sure to fail completely unless the hierarchy shall develop within the immediate future influence sufficient to divide the funds of the public treasury and obtain State support of their sectarian establishments. In the very nature of the republic, such an effort, seriously prosecuted, would mean in the end civil war, for the basis of the nation to-day is its system of universal education linked with universal suffrage.

Romanism in America has therefore received its most serious blow from the American public school.

The two ideals of education involved are utterly irreconcilable. They cannot live on the same soil.

THE PAROCHIAL IDEAL.

What is the ideal of Romanism? If I understand it—something like this: The supreme importance of the catechism, above all literature, art, science, study, culture, abstract or professional. That knowledge is a dangerous power whose sources should be guarded by the sternest repressive measures if necessary, that the human mind shall receive only that which is approved by duly established "authority." That Obedience and Innocence rather than Reason and Character are the goals of culture.

That "secular education," meaning education without the catechism, is immoral and injurious, and therefore worse than ignorance though it may involve the grossest superstitions.

THE STATE IDEAL.

Upon the other hand what is the ideal of the free public school? That the thing of supreme importance is the training of the child's mind to its highest possible powers, leaving the question of religious training to the home and the church. That knowledge is power with freedom and light. That men are free only as they know the truth. That truth is an attribute of God, and to teach truth is to teach God. That therefore all the education in imparting truth is of itself a sacred function. That truth is the one authority and needs no indorsement from its mechanical guardians and that no amount of "authority" can make a lie true. That obedience and innocence are but steps in the growth of man, that the goal of life is Reason and Character. That ignorance is itself the most fertile source of all crime and immorality. That universal education is an absolute necessity to the life of a nation whose sovereignty rests on universal suffrage, and that the State only, is able and willing to give this universal culture and therefore it will brook no rival.

The conflict between these two ideals is irrepressible. They cannot both be true. They cannot both survive in the struggle of our national life to incarnate itself in its perfected form. No man whose mind is unobscured by sectarian fog can believe for one moment that the State will now yield this solemn obligation to defend its own life. No church is willing or able to give universal education to a people. But one church, the Roman Catholic, has ever had the opportunity in having absolute control of the whole population of a nation. What did Rome do with this opportunity? Ask the republics of South America that grope in the darkness of an ignorance well-nigh universal. Ask France if her people were given universal culture until the new State undertook it. Ask Spain the pioneer of New Worlds in the great centuries of the past, ever faithful to Rome, and her ignorant populace will not be slow in giving an emphatic negative. Ask Italy the mother of art and letters, and her millions of ignorant people in their stammering answer mock the glory of her past.

The American nation is bound to maintain her scheme of universal culture to insure her internal peace. Our task is an unique one in history. We must form an amalgam of all the sects, cults, creeds, races, and nationalities of the earth. The public school is the patriotic furnace in which this bleeding of national character is made. Sectarian schools perpetuate the prejudices and differences of our people. To encourage them even would be suicidal for the state.

THE CHILD'S BIRTHRIGHT.

An education being the birthright of every child the state is the only power clothed with authority to protect the child from the brute instincts of unfaithful parentage. The period of infancy in man is the longest by far of all universal life. It lasts about twenty-one years. This prolonged period of infancy is the basis of the human soul. It is the one thing that differentiates man from the animal world by a fathomless chasm. Here lies the secret of humanity. The fact of infancy entitles every child to training. To this end was he born a man and not a brute. The state must guarantee this birthright by its universal and incontestible power—no parent or church should be allowed the right to infringe upon this national right, abridge or destroy it.

If you would know the future of this nation look into the faces of the 13,000,000 school children. The state that could abandon these marching hosts of posterity to the whim of priest or private exploitation would be guilty of high treason against humanity.

The best police power that the state can employ is knowledge and true culture. Ignorance is the fertile mother of vice, crime and pauperism. The state best protects itself in teaching the truths of history, economics, sociology, hygiene and philosophy.

THE STATE ONLY CAN TEACH HISTORY.

The free brains of free children is the noblest defense with any nation ever produced. Invulnerable and united within, the nation is yet to be born who could conquer them. Republics have fallen because their citizenship was ignorant and in their ignorance they fell an easy prey to demagogues and tyrants. The public schools is where the citizen king prepares himself for his throne. The truth only can make a man free. The state only can teach truth without sectarian bias, for the state in exclusive of all sects and the state only can be independent in the statement of the truths of history. Any State, which undertakes that solemn duty will give only one side and suppresses the other. Read the following account of the reign of the Tudors contained in a history taught in Roman Catholic parochial schools:

"To make converts, Catholicity has ever appealed to reason; Protestantism, like Mohammedanism, to force and violence. In England and Scotland Protestantism was forced upon the people by fines, imprisonment and death; in Germany and Prussia, Sweden and Norway, the same. In America the Puritans acted in like manner."

Now I would not forget the infamies of Protestant history. There are some dark pages in our record. There were bloody persecutions in the Old World—even Martin Luther was not guiltless. John Calvin consented to the burning of Servetus. Our Puritan ancestors in New England fell first on their knees and then on the Aborigines, and afterwards made it warm for the "witches." Episcopalians whipped the Baptist, imprisoned and banished them in the early history of Virginia. But the trouble with this remarkable book is that while many of these facts are detailed upon, the inexpressible horrors of the savage reign of "Bloody Mary" in England are not mentioned!

And how utterly false is the statement "Catholicity has ever appealed to reason." Read the hellish edict under which Alva marched into the Netherlands in 1550 as a single illustration.

"No one," said the edict, "shall print, write, copy, keep, conceal, sell, buy or give in churches, streets, or other places, any book or writing made by Martin Luther, John Ecolampedius, Ulrich Zwinglius, Martin Bucer, John Calvin, or other heretics reprobated by the Holy Church;...... nor break nor otherwise injure the images of the Holy Virgin or canonize saints;...... nor in his house hold conventicles or illegal gatherings, or be present at such in which the adherents of the above-mentioned heretics teach, baptize, and form conspiraces against the Holy Church and the general welfare......Moreover, we forbid," continues the edict, "all lay persons to converse or dispute concerning the Holy Scripture, openly or secretly, especially on any doubtful or difficult matter, or to read, teach, or expound the Scriptures, unless they have duly studied theology and been approved by some renowned university;......or to preach secretly or openly, or to entertain any of the opinions of the above-mentioned heretics;......on pain, should any one be found to have contravened any of the points above-mentioned, as perturbators of our state and of the general quiet to be punished in the following manner."

And what were these penalties? The men were to die by the sword and the women to be buried alive if they should recant and did not persist in their errors. If they refused to recant and persisted, then they were to be burned alive, and all their property confiscated. Any one who failed to betray a suspective lodged or entertained such, or furnished with food, fire or clothing, were liable to the same fate.

Armed with this decree of hell, Alva marched his army in the Netherlands, and in six years executed, according to its provisions, 18,000 human beings, besides the hosts slain in battle! No, it will not do to allow any sect to teach history. The state only is fit to take the child by the hand, lead him through its centuries of darkness and tears and suffering, and teach him to respect the opinions of his opponent, and in due humility for the past, love his neighbor, while he differs from him in politics or religion.

To teach history is to trace the footprints of God through the centuries.

To teach science is to unfold the laws of God. The true scientific teacher is filled with divine enthusiasm. It is said that Professor Farrar, who occupied the chair of natural philosophy at Harvard University, two-thirds of a century ago, was a man possessed of this enthusiasm for his work and beloved by his pupils, whom he inspired with something of his own spirit.

One day the class entered the lecture-room and found the professor walking backwards and forwards, with kindled eye and working face, holding a ball in his hands. Presently he stopped and confronted the class and exclaimed, suiting the action to the word:

"I toss this ball into the air; the earth rises up to meet it, and the stars bow down to do it reverence."

The teaching of philosophy is likewise a sacred function. Thought is the witness of God in man. The true thinker is the only true Catholic. In thought man becomes one with the Infinite and the Universal.

A FATAL COLLISION.

On encountering this ideal of education entrenched in the very inner fortress of the government of the United States, Romanism with its medieval ideal has met with a fatal collision. It has encountered an absolutely new force in history. It has collided with the van guard of that progress of the century that is to conquer humanity in the twentieth century. It is a collision with the stars in their courses, with light, with science, with history.

What are some of the results?

The practical defeat of the parochial scheme is already acknowledged by the wisest of the hierarchy. The mission of adjustment and reconciliation of Satolli in America means this among other things. Millions of hard-earned dollars of Catholic money have been sunk in weak parochial schools that must perish before the advance of the public system, unless the school fund is divided in the interests of sectarianism. Such a division cannot be accomplished in the nation without a civil war. It is the dream of a fool.

The public school with each succeeding year becomes more and more popular with the whole people. Hundreds of thousands of the most intelligent Catholics are its warmest supporters, and a truly universal education is the certain destiny of our people. Romanism as a system has lost millions of adherents in this liberalizing, broadening process of thought and culture. Their people have learned to think for themselves. As men grow to conscious power, Obedience must yield to Reason. I command my child now, but soon he will grow into the consciousness of his own freedom, and I must put my arms about his and say, "Come my boy, let us reason together." In the childhood of the race the official church might command with good results for untutored man. But the race draws near to its conscious powers of a full grown manhood. Command must yield to persuasion.

The day of authority for truth is gone. The day of truth only for authority is here.

CHAPTER XI.

Goody-Goodism and the Scourge of Christ.

The corruption of the modern city is a threat against the foundations of social order.. The municipal record of New York during the past thirty years has been a nightmare of civilization. But it has not disturbed the slumber of the Protestant churches. It has not even disturbed seriously its individual ministers until the last few years. The Gospel of Jesus Christ in New York has been weakly and ineffectually presented because it has not been preached in its fullness and power. Jesus Christ, on one occasion in His life, took a scourge of cords and cast out of the Temple the sheep and the oxen, poured out the changer's money and overturned their tables. This is a most remarkable scene in the history of the ministry of Christ. It is a scene in which we behold the indignation of Jesus. So vigorous is this expression that the result is physical violence. To some minds of to-day such a scene in the life of Jesus is an impossibility. They refuse to believe in such a Christ, and these are the people who insist that they have the last word from Christ to the world. The trouble is that they have looked only at one aspect of the life of Jesus. He is gentle, He is loving, He is tender, He weeps, and yet deliberately makes a scourge of cords and with physical violence drives from the Temple those who were desecrating His Father's house and with physical violence overturns their tables. Christ is Christianity. Jesus said, "I am the way."

What does this scene in the life of Jesus, directly in the line of His ministry, teach?

Certainly two things.

There is an hour for Christianity to wield the lash and use the knife. There is a time, in other words, for all things. There is a time for gentleness and tenderness and love. There is a time for wrath and indignation and for overturning. There is a time to laugh, there is a time to weep; there is a time to sing, a time to pray, a time to fight. The music of life is not made on a single string. There are other elements than the gentle and soothing, which enter into the essentials of a rounded, active life. It is so in the individual, in society and in the church.

In the life of every man there are times for tenderness and love; there are times for the assertion of the sterner elements of life and the assertion of wrath and indignation at the proper time, as essential to the world's welfare, to the salvation and happiness of mankind, as the introduction and maintenance of the gentler and sweeter elements. No man can live a normal life in this world and do his duty, endowed even with moderate talents, without being confronted with hours in which the soul must rise in all the power of righteous indignation and assert in all their elemental power the forces of anger and of war.

A TIME FOR RIGHTEOUS WRATH.

In the life of society there are times when the community must rise in indignation and rid itself of pestilence. There are times in the life of a community in which the seeds of joy and of love and of gentleness can be sowed and cultivated. But there are hours when, with flame and axe those who have the good of society at heart must go forth and burn and strike down and remove if the people are to be saved from contagion and death. So in the history of the church there are hours in which the gospel of joy and of peace and of loving kindness is preached and should be preached, and there are other hours in which the wrath and indignation of truth and Christ must be preached. It is useless to say that in such an hour light will overcome darkness, gentleness will overcome violence. Jesus Christ did not find it so. His disciples would do well to follow Him. There have been hours in almost every century of the history of the church in which there was absolute call for righteous wrath, and when only such forces were adequate to the salvation of the church and of the people.

What could have saved the church in the days of Martin Luther save the violence which resulted in the Protestant establishment and in the purification of the Catholic Church? There could be no compromise with the corruption that had grown up within the body of Roman Catholicism. Tetzel, the chief exponent of the doctrine of indulgence, preached in the ear of Luther. "Indulgences," said he, "are the most precious and sublime of God's gifts. This cross (pointing to the red cross) has as much efficacy as the cross of Jesus Christ. Draw near, and I will give you letters duly sealed by which even the sins you shall hereafter desire to commit shall be forgiven you. I would not exchange my privileges for those of St. Peter in heaven, for I have saved more souls with my indulgences than he with his sermons. There is no sin so great that the indulgence cannot reach it. Let him only pay largely, and it shall be forgiven him. Even repentance is not indispensable."

If any man doubts that this be a true statement of the preaching of a duly accredited delegate from the highest Catholic authority in his age, let him refer to the words of Pope Adrian, successor to Leo X., crowned in 1522, when Germany was ablaze with Lutheranism. Through his legate the Pope declared at the diet of Nuremberg, summoned to deal with Luther, that "these disorders had sprung from the sins of men, more especially from the sins of priests and prelates. Even in the holy chair," said he, "many horrible crimes have been committed. The contagious disease, spreading from the head to the members, from the Pope to lesser prelates, has spread far and wide, so that scarcely any one is found who does right and is free from infection." Confronted with such a situation, can say sane man maintain that it was the duty of Martin Luther to remain quiet and to preach the simple gospel of love and gentleness, of good feeling to friends and enemies inside the church and outside? No; there was an hour in which the honest soul of the reformer cried in hot indignation, "In the name of Jesus, I will endure it no longer!" and the issue of battle was joined. There is a time to pray. There is a time to fight.

THE TERRORS OF DEVOTED LOVE.

True love in Christ has its terrible hours in such a world. There are aspects of love beyond the mere expression of tenderness and of kindly feeling. Love has its hours of the terrible and of the sublime, when death is preferable to dishonor, and when violence is to be desired above the baser things that come with submission. A Virginius could kill his own child for love's sake, and we cannot say that the awful deed of such a father transcended the limits of the real expression of a father's love. Let us remember that Jesus was not only capable of anger, but that He was angry. If this be so, love living in this world must be confronted with hours in which wrath and indignation rule supreme. It cannot be otherwise. The love which filled the soul of Christ was a consuming fire, and before it evil must be burned up.

We are told that His baptism was the baptism of the Holy Ghost and of fire. Upon more than one occasion in His life we are told that He was angry. He said Himself that He came to bring not peace, but a sword. Such scenes in the life of Jesus, such utterances from his lips, cannot be reconciled with the sentimental slush of a certain school of Christianity which continues to cry "peace, peace," when there is no peace, when there can be no peace with the forces of hell. There is a large amount of unadulterated hypocrisy in the cry for the gentleness of the Gospel in this hour. It will be found in scores of cases to emanate from men who hate the Gospel of Christ with all their soul and who cry for the gentleness and its sweetness because they feel the touch of the sword of Christ, of His truth and His indignation and His anger in their inmost souls.

Jesus sacrificed Himself. Christianity means the sacrifice of self. If we would be the disciples of Christ, we must be willing

108 GOODY-GOODISM AND THE SCOURGE OF CHRIST.

to sacrifice self. The man who sacrifices himself must displease the selfish. It is an arraignment of them and of their life. One of the most difficult sacrifices for the follower of Christ to make to-day is to count his reputation as nothing for Christ's sake; is to be willing to be hissed and cursed and spit on by the people. The most difficult sacrifice which Christianity demands of its followers to-day is that they be willing to be unpopular. It is an easy thing to pander to a vitiated public sentiment. It is an easy thing to sell one's soul for this cheap applause. The follower of Christ who does it has betrayed his Master, has belied his profession and is untrue to the first principles of his life—the sacrifice of self.

The world hated Jesus Christ. He was not a popular preacher in the sense that he pleased the powers that rule society. It is impossible for any man to live a true Christian life in this world, following Jesus in spirit and in truth and not be hated. Jesus says it Himself in so many words. Hear Him: "If ye were of the world, the world would love its own. But because ye are not of the world, but I chose you out of the world, therefore the world hateth you. They persecuted me. They will also persecute you. Yea, the hour cometh that whosoever killeth you shall think he offereth service unto God."

THE SWORD OF CHRISTIANITY.

There is and there must be of necessity a point of contact with evil at which Christianity bursts into a consuming flame. The Christianity, incapable of such a consummation, of such violence, if you please, is dead, not living. Nor is this in any wise inconsistent with the highest conception of Jesus. In His personality was blended the tenderest, the divinest love, with all the elements of sternest, moral warfare. We see these elements combined frequently in the character of the stern warrior. Prince Henry, the brother of Frederick the Great, King of Prussia, leads his army through Saxony, upon mission of death, and yet

GOODY-GOODISM AND THE SCOURGE OF CHRIST. 109

he is careful of every field of grain. If a soldier stepped out of the direct road, the captain was punished.

One day in the harvest season the prince saw the peasants hurrying to save their crops from an approaching storm. Immediately he had every horse taken from the baggage wagons and sent to the assistance of the farmers, who were amazed at this sympathy from a great general and an enemy. On one occasion 300 French officers were taken prisoners and brought before him. He was indignant that they had been deprived of their swords and restored them at once. The wounded among the prisoners he cared for as carefully as if they belonged to his own army. When he learned that fifty of them were without money, he provided for them from his own purse, and at considerable inconvenience to himself. It is possible to fight for principle and truth and right, and in the very battle seek the salvation of those against whom we fight.

And after these wars for righteous principles it happens, again and again in the history of the world, that those against whom we fight are brought to see that they were wrong, and that the battle was for their own good, even though they were blind and could not see it. We have a most striking example of this result in a remarkable confession made by Arabi Pasha, the Egypt patriot. Twelve years ago he was the most powerful man in Egypt. He headed a rebellion, nominally, against the Khedive, but which Arabi insisted was really on the Khedive's behalf. He desired, he said, to deliver Egypt from foreign domination and preserve her for the Egyptians. He made a brave and desperate fight, but he was beaten, and has since been living in retirement in Ceylon. He declares that his interest in Egypt and love for his country, are as intense as ever. He declared recently that his whole life had been a mistake. He regretted opposing the English occupation of Egypt. He declared that he had found the English had done for his country what he had hoped to do, but could never have succeeded in doing.

"Not one of her own sons," said Arabi, "could have given

Egypt the release from oppression and injustice and the good government which she now enjoys. All that I have fought and struggled to attain is accomplished. In my blindness I was resisting the surest means of achieving my own aims. I was fighting for the liberation of my country. I am sorry now I did so, and I am glad for my country's sake I was defeated." So the men against whom Christianity wages its righteous war will in the end rejoice in their own defeat. Such a war is waged against them, not because we hate them, but because we love them.

THE POLLUTION OF MODERN CITIES.

So to-day the church of Christ in our centres of civic life is confronted with just such a crisis. The hour has come for righteous indignation. It is the hour for righteous wrath and for the action—yes, the violence of the Christ under the influence of that wrath. This is so:—

Because of the tremendous growth and importance of these great modern centres of life. The city is the heart of modern civilization. It is the key to the century. It is the key to the future. The past fifty years have seen the city grow to dominate the world. It has drained the life from the rural districts and concentrated it at these nerve centres of the world. Here civilization has massed its numbers. The cities of the ancient world, before the fall of that world, were insignificant in comparison with the giant cities of the close of the nineteenth century.

Imperial Rome, mistress of the ancient world, was a pigmy beside London, the capital of the modern world. And London of to-day is but a faint prophecy of what will be the London of the close of the twentieth century, at the present rate of progress. Here in the city is concentrated the wealth of the nation, the wealth of the world. Money, and all the power of money, and all that money means to society, to commerce, to politics, to the masses, to the race, are to be settled here. The influence of the city is now absolutely supreme as the governing power. The city governs our politics, state and national. The city governs the commerce of the world, national and international. The city governs the formation of the social structure; it governs fashions; it rules literature; it controls the press; it makes the atmosphere which those who rule the nation breathe.

While the growth and importance of the city have been thus overwhelming and continuous to increase with incredible swiftness, it is precisely in the city that the failure of the church has been most pitiful. Taking the modern world as a whole, Christianity has made remarkable progress within the past quarter of a century. In America Christianity has advanced with rapid strides, taking the country as a whole. We have enrolled 20,000,000 adherents in the United States. We have thousands of churches. We are building thousands of new ones every year. Church membership has increased in larger proportion than the population. Christianity is triumphant along the line, reckoning things in their total.

Our progress in the heathen world has been miraculous. Closed gates have opened wide. Nations have been baptized in a day. The ports of the earth are now open to the Christian missionary, and their triumphs have been miraculous. But here our boast must end, and our sorrow begin. This increase has been in the small towns. It has been in the country. In the city we have not only failed to increase, but Christianity has perceptibly declined in its organic life within the past generation.

HEATHENISM IN OUR CITIES.

The old Twentieth Assembly District in New York had a population of 60,000 and there were three little Protestant churches. In the whole nation for every 60,000 there are 120 Evangelical churches. But there is one district in New York with 50,000 souls in which there is one Protestant Church. In the heart of Chicago there are 60,000 people, it is said, without a single church, either Protestant or Catholic. In six assembly districts of New York there is a population of 360,000 people, for which there are 31 Protestant churches, and 3,018 saloons. The whole country east of the Mississippi shows that there are as many churches as saloons, and yet for this population in New York, larger than the city of Cincinnati, there are 100 times as many saloons as churches. The First Assembly District of New York in 1880 had 44,000 people, 7 Protestant Churches, and 1,072 saloons—153 saloons for every church.

Nor does this failure of church life simply apply to Protestantism. Our Jewish population has become atheistic and have deserted their synagogues by thousands. At an Ingersoll lecture one-half the audience will be found composed of Jews, and it is a remarkable fact that sometimes whole families will be found at these Sabbath entertainments over which the distinguished Colonel presides.

The truth is the city of to-day, the modern city, whether in the East or in the West, is a hell, in which the manhood of the nation is daily being consumed. Materialism is rampant. The god of the city is the god of mammon. More and more have the stong fallen into this fetich worship. Their motto is "Money, by all means, by any means, fair or foul." The hot breath of this scourge soon burns out the ideals, the faiths, the hopes and the love born into the heart of man under normal conditions. The sum total of the forces that affect life in our cities to-day is overwhelmingly against the development of a righteous character. The pressure of work is insane. Men are in a fever. They do not stop to think. Things high and holy and noble are brushed aside in the mad scramble of the modern business world. Men are driven to such an intense speed that the moral point of view is lost. The reaction from this results in dissipation rather than amusement.

In the reaction from this debauchery of body and soul sane amusement seems almost an impossibility; hence the degradation of our amusements in the cities to-day. Our theatres wallow in filth. They pander to the gutter. They pander to the Bowery. They pander to the vicious in high society and in low society, and there is scarcely an exception. Gambling is rampant and opens its thousand doors to allure the young and to absolutely destroy. In this pressure of life the social evil is intensified. Womanhood in degradation becomes a power for evil. Saloons have multiplied not only in numbers, but in their power for evil, in their attractions, until it is next to impossible for a man with honest intentions in the lower walks of life to live in a modern city and keep out of these hell-holes.

VILE LITERATURE IN OUR CITIES.

The reading matter which is provided for this population is of the most degraded character. It is thrust under the nose of the passing crowd. It is nailed upon the bulletins in glaring colors. It is circulated among the young and the foolish, the ignorant and the thoughtless, to bear its fruit of death from day to day.

The influence in the higher circles of society is irrational,materialistic, and tends to destroy reverence, faith and the stability of home and home ideals. The people in our cities live in tenements, live in overcrowded hovels, in which dogs and hogs could not breathe, and exist through many generations. It is simply a physical impossibility for rational manhood and womanhood to be born and reared in such houses, in such streets, and under such conditions as exist in our modern cities. This fact is shown in the deterioration of the working people.

It was found recently in London by an investigation, that the "submerged tenth" of the population was not the rural population, which had come into London, but it was the population born in London under modern conditions. The countrymen who come in to fill the lower walks of life in our cities contain enough vigorous blood to fight their way over the bodies of the weaker men and women of the city. Official corruption grows apace in such a life. In the midst of this the church is corrupted by the power of the rich and conservative, and is asleep with its traditions.

I am not a pessimist. I do not believe in the triumph of evil.

I have not drawn this dark picture because I am in despair, but we must face the fact. The city to-day is destroying the character and the manhood of the nation. The modern city as at present constituted does not produce men and women capable of really fighting the battles of life seriously and to a successful issue. The modern city cannot exist but for the blood that pours into it from our rural districts, and this blood is consumed from day to day in this fiery furnace of a corrupt and corrupting life. You cannot point out to me to-day in a single great city of America a solitary man born under the conditions of modern city life whose influence counts for much in this nation's life.

Phillips Brooks was born in Boston, but he was born in Boston fifty years ago, and Boston was a straggling country village at that time as compared with the Boston of to-day. The modern city, as at present constituted, does not produce men. It cannot produce men. If they are born within it, they cannot be reared to vigorous manhood. The forces that destroy character are overwhelming as compared with the forces that build character. The doors that open to destruction are a hundred to one that open for life. I do not believe that there has been enough manhood born and reared in our modern cities within the past generation to save a single one of them from hell for twenty-four hours, if that salvation depended upon the capacity of that manhood for organization, for direction, for production.

DANGERS OF THE MODERN CITY.

I am not a pessimist, but facts are facts. I believe in the race, I believe in its future—but what race? The modern city threatens the future of our nation's life. The smoke and fumes, full of disease and of sin and death, that rise to-day from these great centres of our life, form a cloud whose threatening storm must burst upon the nation in the future. That which is worthy to live will live. Truth will triumph. God will reign supreme. The question is, Will you be in that triumph?

I believe that the hour is come in which Christian manhood in

GOODY-GOODISM AND THE SCOURGE OF CHRIST. 115

these rapidly developing centres must take a firm stand and draw the sword of the righteousness of Christ and defend its strongholds if we are to save the people. Mothers write me from country towns to look after their boys and save them. I tell you it is next to impossible. The forces that tend to destroy character in New York City are 100 to 1. We fight against an army that is overwhelming, and we fight with children's toys. We are playing with issues, and our enemies laugh at us in our helplessness. With our delicate white ties and our clerical-cut clothes we are trifling with the great question of the salvation of the people, of a generation, of a race. There are times when Christian manhood should take a firm stand. Only in such a stand can the people be saved. Our enemies are incapable of persuasion. The devil in the modern city is a Turk in spirit.

Sir Charles Euan-Smith, the recent British envoy to Fez, in the Empire of Morocco, had a perilous experience in the Anti-Christian riot. The mission house had been attacked. The windows were smashed with stones. It became unsafe to venture in the gardens. As Sir Charles was giving the necessary orders for the defense of the mission an embassy from the Sultan appeared and implored him to go at once to the palace. Courier after courier, mounted on magnificent Barbary horses, dashed up, repeating the summons. Bending at his feet, they declared, "My lord, we pray thee to listen. Our lord beseeches that you come to him. He will neither eat nor drink nor sleep nor have any peace until you come to him. Our lord languisheth for the light of your countenance." No less than twenty of these messengers delivered their dramatic summons on the way.

The Sultan met Sir Charles in great agitation. "Your life is in danger," he said. "Your wife and your people must come immediately to the palace. The populace is greatly excited against you. I can no longer protect you. Come to-night and sleep here. In the morning I will send a thousand soldiers to escort you to the coast." "Your majesty is mistaken," replied Sir Charles coolly. "My life is not in danger. I am in your majesty's safe keeping." "I am powerless to protect you," cried the Sultan. "If you return to the mission you will be killed." "Perhaps I am to be killed," replied Sir Charles. "The mission may be massacred, but there will be another British minister in Fez within a month, who will be accompanied by a staff as well equipped as mine and better, for," added the minister in deliberate tones, "then there will not be a Sultan at Fez."

It is needless to say that Sir Charles and the mission were protected. The men who were responsible for the riots were beaten and imprisoned. The Pasha who urged the mob to stone the British vice-consul was fined $10,000. He crawled on foot and placed the money at Minister Smith's feet. He swore on the Koran he had not incited the riot. His guards were flogged before the palace, and Minister Smith gave the money to the poor of Fez and rewarded his faithful servants and soldiers.

FACE SATAN IN HIS STRONGHOLD.

So the soldier of to-day has but to face the devil in his stronghold and the victory will be his. The hour has come, if the future of the city is to be Christian, when we must overturn and overturn, and with scourge and sword drive out the forces that now make life impossible. The prophecy which Dr. Strong uttered in 1885 to-day rings in our ears with more startling emphasis than when he first gave it utterance. It is well to read it again. Referring to the inevitable crisis which the forces of evil are bringing to pass in our modern cities, he says:

"When such a commercial crisis has closed factories by the ten thousand and wage earners have been thrown out of employment by the million; when the public lands, which hitherto at such times have afforded relief, are all exhausted; when our urban population has been multiplied several fold, and our Cincinnatis have become Chicagos, our Chicagos New Yorks, and our New Yorks Londons; when class antipathies are deepened; when socialistic organizations, armed and drilled, are in every city, and the ignorant and vicious power of crowded populations has fully found itself; when the corruption of city government is grown apace; when crops fail, or some gigantic 'corner' doubles the price of bread; with starvation in the home; with idle workmen gathered, sullen and desperate, in the saloons; with unprotected wealth at hand; with the tremendous forces of chemistry within easy reach, then, with the opportunity, the means, the fit agents, the motive, the temptation to destroy, all brought into evil conjunction, then will come the real test of our institutions; then will appear whether we are capable of government.

CHAPTER XII.

The Religion of the Future.

Does the decay of Protestantism in New York indicate the fact that religion in general is on the decline? I do not believe it. There are those who assert it. There are those who assert that religion belongs to the childhood of the race. That as man grows to the stature of intellectual maturity, religion ceases to be a necessity. He consequently abandons the temples of the fathers. That this development is inevitable, resistless, means the abolition at last of all forms of worship. I do not believe that this is true. It is simply an assumption that is not borne out by the facts. I believe, besides, it is an assumption born in the peculiarly personal equation of the man who asserts it.

Religion is fundamental to man's nature. He can no more escape its necessity than he can jump out of his own skin. Religion is the effort in man to rise to that which is higher, upon the sacrifice of self. It is in the very nature of man thus to strive. If a man call himself an infidel, his religion is his infidelity. It becomes to him his cause, his purpose, his aim in life, the means by which he seeks to rise to the divine above himself. The most enthusiastic dogmatists in the world are so-called free-thinkers. Mrs. Besant stumped England as an infidel. She has now become a Hindoo; boasts she has a white body, but a black soul. It simply means that religion is fundamental to our very natures.

PROGRESSION.

Therefore, the religion of the future will be progressive. It will be progressive because it will be vital. Progress is the law of life. An attempt to embalm religion means its death. The

religion of the future will welcome progress. The reason why there are so few men in the churches of New York to-day, is that the church has ceased to be progressive. Women outnumber men, four to one, in our decaying church-life—why? Because the feminine temperament is essentially conservative. Woman is the conservator of the race. All radicalism is essentially masculine, all conservatism essentially feminine. Woman, therefore, does not rebel as does man, at the failure to go forward, to create new forms, new thoughts, new methods. Christ Himself declared that He had many things to say unto His disciples, but that the time was not ripe; they could not bear them. "Howbeit," said He, "when the Spirit of truth is come he will lead you into the whole truth." In one sense, therefore, the Catholic Church is more in line with the church of the future than Protestantism. The Catholic Church believes in a progressive revelation, in the ever-living Spirit within the church. Herein Roman Catholicism is right and Protestantism wrong, for this is the re-echo of the promise of Jesus Christ.
Number Eighteen

SIMPLICITY.

The religion of the future must be a simple, as contrasted with a formal, religion. Jesus was a form-breaker. He broke the Sabbath day, He ate with publicans and sinners, He ate with unwashed hands. This was a violation of the fundamentals of the ritual of the church of His fathers. The growth of the intellect of man is coincident with the decay of forms. Forms are for those who feel the need of them. The younger the intellectual development, the stronger is this feeling of need. The religion that holds the thinkers of the next century will not be formal, but simple. Out of forty-three governors of the States of this Union, only seventeen of them are members of the church; yet every one of them profess heart allegiance to the religion of Jesus. This means that the men of force and of character and of individuality, more and more will be disassociated from the mere formalities of church-life, unless the requirements of those forms are made less stringent and less essential.

IN HARMONY WITH REASON.

The religion of the future will be in harmony with reason, with history, with intelligence. Therefore, the clergyman of the future will own a study, a library, not a shop in which he manufactures sermons. He may be charged with tendencies that are heretical. Any man that studies must doubt. Doubt is the beginning of knowledge. No man ever learned anything except through the vestibule of a doubt. The man who is afraid of a doubt is dead intellectually. Religion must be in harmony with the divine light of Reason. I mean by Reason the sum total of man's spiritual faculties, including conscience. God has given man Reason as the primal light which lights every man coming into the world. Reason does not clash with faith; rather it is the complement of faith. When Reason has gone to its farthest limit, faith reaches forward into the darkness and cries, "I believe!" Any religion that clashes with the light of Reason is a superstition, not religion. We cannot, in other words, believe what we know to be a lie to be the truth. Any man who says that he can believe a lie to be true is simply declaring himself to be a liar. There can be no clash between Reason and religion. Whenever there is a clash it simply means that what we call religion is the sheerest superstition. A British critic, in reviewing the work of a professor of theology in America, entitled "Orthodoxy and Heterodoxy," says, concerning his attitude to the criticism of Scripture: "It is devoid of intelligence to the extent of being immoral to a man occupying his position." We cannot longer teach traditions as the essence of faith. If we teach the doctrine of the Trinity it must be a rational doctrine, or it will not be held by the dawning century. The Trinity taught in the past has been a bald tri-theism instead of a Trinity, and the error came simply from the Latin translation of the Bible. The word persona meant, in the Latin, the mask through which the actor speaks. God in three persons, in the Latin, meant God speaking through three characters on the stage—one God, therefore, speaking through the mask of Father, Son, Spirit. We have lost the meaning of the word persona in our word person. Our word person means the individual. Persona meant the mask through which the individual speaks. One person, therefore, could speak through many masks—so one God speaks through three characters. This faith harmonizes with the light of reason. Such must be the reconstruction of the traditions of our theology.

DEEDS NOT CREEDS.

When we worship God we must not worship the devil. We cannot define God to be a fiend and call Him good. Upon such traditions the conscience of humanity has outgrown orthodoxy. The only worship of the religion of the Father must be the worship which Christ demanded of His Disciples, namely, the service of man. "The Son of man came not to be ministered unto, but to minister." "As the Father hath sent me, even so I send you." And I believe that the Church will triumph in the centuries—but what Church? I do not mean by this any ecclesiastical establishment that claims the glories of historic record. I mean the Church of Jesus Christ—the Christianity of Christ as distinguished from the Christianity of ecclesiastical history. The characteristic of that triumphant Church will certainly be that its standard will be ethical, not theoretical. The Christian world is already a unit on ethics, Christianity is divided on the subject of government and a few abstract doctrines. There is no division as to the essential ethical code. As to deeds we are already one. Our code, the world over, is the Ten Commandments—love to God and love to man. The Greek Church declares that only this man truly has religion. The Latin Church declares that only this man is a true worshipper. The Protestant Church declares that only the man who complies with the requirements of this code is a true disciple of Christ. Whatever men may profess, to whatever creed or church they may belong, there is but one standard of ethics, to-day for the Christian world, and it is the same standard for every division of Christendom. This will undoubtedly be the first corner-stone of the great Church that will triumph in the future—the essentiality of deeds rather than creeds.

SAM JONES AND EMERSON.

The men who succeed, to-day, in winning the world to their religion are precisely the men whatever be their forms of expression, who preach, distinctly and forcefully, an ethical gospel. I have heard men of the world say that they were disgusted with the vulgarity of Sam Jones and wonder why he can succeed in reaching and holding and converting to righteousess thousands of his fellow men. I have heard ministers who prided themselves upon their orthodoxy wonder at Sam Jones's success for another reason. They said, "He does not preach Christ," does not preach the Atonement, the blood; and they marvel at his success. There is but one reason for this wonderful man's success, and that is, with all the peculiarities of his methods, he preaches with tremendous earnestness the fundamentals of an ethical religion, whose unceasing refrain is, "Quit your meanness." This is simply the vernacular translation of the message of Christ: "Not every one that sayeth unto me 'Lord, Lord,' shall enter in; but he that doeth the will of my Father." B. Fay Mills is another of our successful evangelists. I have known him to hold meetings in large cities in which the entire business of the community was suspended at noon-day to attend the services. This thing occurs not once or twice; but it has occurred hundreds of times, and it has occurred in almost every State of the Union. What is the secret of Mr. Mills's power? I believe it is simply this—he preaches, with tremendous earnestness, a profoundly ethical gospel. Why is it that Ralph Waldo Emerson, though disassociated from any church, possesses a peculiar power over the minds of this generation? He is a teacher of tremendous power.

THE RELIGION OF THE FUTURE.

There is scarcely a young man or woman of culture in any Protestant denomination in New England and the Middle States who is not influenced more or less by this great teacher's words. Why has he this power? He teaches the fundamentals of an ethical faith.

That is to say, if you take away from the Christianity of Christendom all that reason and conscience condemns or questions, you will have remaining the simple Christianity of Christ. His religion was a religion of conduct. He never uttered a faith He di d not rest on it Himself. He breathed no hope that was not His own. And when He spoke of faith He did not mean assent to a dogma; He meant personal devotion to Himself. No teacher in the world ever said less about creeds than Jesus Christ. His burden was human life. He laid down no dogmas, invented no formularies, made no fine definitions.

Upon the other hand, the Church, in its ecclesiastical development, has been busy discussing abstract and difficult problems that are of no importance on this earth, beneath it or above it. For hundreds of years the ecclesiastics fought like tigers over the letter "I" in a Greek word, and knew no more when they got through with the discussion than they did when they began. The Christian Church was divided into the Greek and Latin divisions by what is called the filioque clause of the Nicene Creed; that is, whether the Holy Ghost proceeds from the Father and the Son, or from the Father alone—and what this means God in heaven only knows. Christ certainly made no reference to any such nonsensical discussions. His commands were simple, personal, vital. "Love one another." "My commandment is that ye love one another." "Inasmuch as ye did it; enter. Inasmuch as ye did it not, depart." The salvation of conduct and of character is the only salvation about which Jesus Christ ever spoke.

HUMANITARIAN.

The religion of the future in the Church triumphant will be humanitarian and it will be humane. It will not, because it cannot, damn a world to save a syllogism. The enlightened conscience of humanity will not tolerate it. It can only take Calvin and Tertullian in broken doses. It will take so much of the orthodoxy of the past as can be reconciled with the enlightened Christian conscience of humanity. It will modify, therefore, those exaggerations of truth that violate conscience. "I have sinned," said Martin Luther, "but Christ has not sinned; sin, sin mightily, but have all the more confidence in Christ. We are justified by God, gratis. He imputes righteousness to us, which makes us directly holy as though we were altogether without sin." In the exaggeration of this doctrine the Reformation will have to be reformed. John Calvin speaks of the delightful benefits of the predestination of the damned. Tertullian, one of the fathers, said: "The sweetest music of heaven will be the wailings of the lost." A Christian minister is reported to have said in his pulpit, a few years ago: "My hearers, you may imagine that when you are in heaven and look down upon your friends in hell, your happiness will be somewhat marred. Not a bit of it. By that time you will be so purified and perfected, that as you gaze upon that sea of suffering it will only increase your joy." Such stuff as this is the vapid raving of insanity, and the enlightened conscience of the human race has long ago utterly repudiated it. If this be orthodoxy, the religion of the future is certain to be heterodox.

SAVING POWER.

This Church triumphant will have only one mark of its authority, and that will be its power to save men. That is the only authority which Christ promised. "Ye are the salt of the earth. If the salt have lost its savor it will be cast out and trodden under foot of men." If it saves, then it is a salt. The church that saves is the Church of Christ. The church that gets frightened by a mob of unwashed, abandoned people, folds up its tent and sneaks off uptown to find a soft place to live, has already lost its savor and is fit only to be trampled under the foot of men. It is useless for such an organiaztion to prate about historic authority or historic continuity. The supreme test is the power to lift up man and save him—save him, soul and body, for the ministry of Jesus was both to the body and the soul. His ministry of healing forms a large part of the record of H's life.

A SOCIAL POWER.

This triumphant Church must be a social power. It must preach a sociological as contradistinguished from a merely individual gospel. Man, to-day, is more than an individual. The individual has played his part in the development of the centuries. This age is a social age, the age of federation, the age of organization, of solidarity, of humanity. "No man liveth to himself." A gospel that is a vital one, to-day, must touch business, it must touch labor, it must touch capital. It must lay its hand upon politics, which is but religion in action. It must know that the state is merely the organ of the whole people which they use in their pursuit of righteousness. That the state is a function, therefore, of the Christian Church that is to conquer the world. That ecclesiastical power can never supplant this power, because it is in itself more sacred than the ecclesiastic.

COMMON SENSE.

Its methods must be the methods of common sense; therefore, they will be simple. When Paul went to Athens as a preacher, he did not go to the little Jewish synagogue, the church of his fathers, and simply say: "I am here to preach the Gospel of Jesus Christ. I preach it to you, and if you don't believe it you can go to hell. My duty is done." He went down into the market-place, he went to the acropolis where the Athenians went to congregate, to discuss the news. He rose before them, discoursed to them about their art, about their literature, their poets and sculptors, and, skilfully gaining their attention and interest, told them about the monument he had observed to an unknown God. This was the entering wedge through which he poured his message of love from Christ. In Athens, he was an Athenian.

Among every people he was all things to all men, if by all means he might save some. The church of the future, therefore, will not be afraid of sensationalism.

This church must be honest with men. If there are clerical errors in the Bible it cannot contradict the results of the scholarship of the centuries and expect to live. It must accept these results. As a great scholar has so truthfully said: "The whole system of traditional orthodoxy, Greek, Latin and Protestant, must progress or it will be left behind the age and lose its hold on thinking men. The church must keep pace with civilization, adjust herself to the modern conditions of religious and political freedom, and accept the established results of Biblical and historical criticism and natural science. God speaks in history and science as well as in the Bible and the church, and He cannot contradict Himself. Truth is sovereign, and must and will prevail over all ignorance, error and prejudice." And, therefore, the present church will be adapted to the environment of its new life. Want of adaptation means death. As a great preacher in England has recently said: "Institutions can only continue to exist by adapting themselves to their surroundings. Now the church, as we have seen, is quite out of harmony with modern civilization. Both morally and intellectually it is centuries behind the age. The most highly educated people have discarded the fundamental doctrines of orthodoxy. Even the average man is beginning to look upon those doctrines with suspicion and contempt. They are opposed to the best instincts of the race, instincts which are becoming every day more authoritative. The church is bound, therefore, to be either reformed or destroyed. If it is not reformed from within it will be destroyed from without. And by reform I do not mean any patching up of the Articles, any tinkering of the Creeds. It must be a thorough, radical, absolute reform. It must begin again from the beginning. It must take a fresh start from Christ. The last two thousand years of ecclesiastical nightmare must be as though they had never been. The church must be born again."

This church must, therefore, have a ministry of power. The men who shall belong to this ministry must be ordained of God, not of man. They must have the primal endowments of a resistless personality. The standard of the man now applying to enter the ministry is below the average of the intellectual attainments of this generation. There are a thousand preachers around this city to-day, therefore, out of a job. They have missed their calling. Their real function should have been the development of agriculture. When a church vacancy occurs these men literally fall over one another in the scramble to get the place. The day for this sort of minister is gone. Men only of personal, intellectual power can expect to live in the church of the future.

TRUTH IN ALL.

This glorious church of the future must be honest with church history, and, therefore, it must be liberal in spirit. It must recognize the truth wherever it is found, and return thanks to God for every aspect of truth presented by the different developments of historic Christianity. It must accept with joy the magnificent summary of church history made by that matchless historian, Dr. Schaff, just before his death. Hear him:

"The Greek Church is a glorious church: for in her language have come down to us the oracles of God, the Septuagint, the Gospels, and Epistles; hers are the early confessors and martyrs, the Christian fathers, bishops, patriarchs and emperors; here the immortal writings of Origen, Eusebius, Athanasius and Chrysostom; here the Oecumenical Councils and the Nicene Creed, which can never die.

"The Latin Church is a glorious church; for she carried the treasures of Christian and classical literature over the gulf of the migration of nations and preserved order in the chaos of civil wars; she was the Alma Mater of the barbarians of Europe; she turned painted savages into civilized beings and worshippers of idols into worshippers of Christ; she built up the colossal structures of the papal theocracy, the canon law, the monastic orders, the cathedrals and the universities; she produced the profound systems of scholastic and mystic theology; she stimulated and patronized the Renaissance, the printing press and the discovery of a new world; she still stands, like an immovable rock, bearing witness to the fundamental truths and facts of our holy religion, and to the Catholicity, unity, unbroken continuity and independence of the church; and she is as zealous as ever in missionary enterprise and self-denying works of Christian charity.

"We hail the Reformation, which redeemed us from the yoke of spiritual despotism and secured us religious liberty—the most precious of all liberties—and made the Bible, in every language, a book for all classes and conditions of men.

"The Evangelical Lutheran Church, the first-born daughter of the Reformation, is a glorious Church: for she set the Word of God above the traditions of men, and bore witness to the comforting truth of justification by faith; she struck the keynote to thousands of sweet hymns in praise of the Redeemer; she is boldly and reverently investigating the problems of faith and philosophy and is constantly making valuable additions to theological lore.

"The Evangelical Reformed Church is a glorious Church: for she carried the Reformation from the Alps and lakes of Switzerland 'to the end of the West' (to use the words of the Roman Clement about St. Paul); she furnished more martyrs of conscience in France and the Netherlands alone than any other church, even during the first three centuries; she educated heroic races, like the Huguenots, the Dutch, the Puritans, the Covenanters, the Pilgrim Fathers, who, by the fear of God, were raised above the fear of tyrants, and lived and died for the advancement of civil and religious liberty; she is rich in learning and good works of faith: she keeps pace with all true progress; she grapples with the problems and evils of modern society; and she sends the Gospel to the ends of the earth.

"The Episcopal Church of England, the most churchly of the reformed family, is a glorious Church: for she gave to the English-speaking world the best version of the Holy Scriptures and the best prayer-book: she preserved the order and dignity of the ministry and public worship; she nursed the knowledge and love of antiquity and enriched the treasury of Christian literature; and, by the Anglo-Catholic revival, under the moral, intellectual and poetic leadership of three shining lights of Oxford—Pusey, Newman and Keble—she infused new life into her institutions and customs, and prepared the way for a better understanding between Anglicanism and Romanism.

"The Presbyterian Church of Scotland, the most flourishing daughter of Geneva—as John Knox, 'who never feared the face of man,' was the most faithful disciple of Calvin—is a glorious Church: for she turned a barren country into a garden, and raised a poor and semi-barbarous people to a level with the richest and most intelligent nations; she diffused the knowledge of the Bible and a love of the kirk in the huts of the peasant as well as the places of the nobleman;she has always stood up for church order and discipline, for the rights of the laity, and,first and last, for the crown-rights of King Jesus, which are above all earthly crowns, even that of the proudest monarch on whose dominion the sun never sets.

"The Congregational Church is a glorious Church: for she has taught the principle and proved the capacity, of congregational independence and self-government, based upon a living faith in Christ, without diminishing the effect of voluntary co-operation in the Master's service; and has laid the foundation of New England with its literary and theological institutions and high social culture.

"The Baptist Church is a glorious Church: for she bore, and still bears, testimony to the primitive mode of baptism, to the purity of the congregation, to the separation of church and state and the liberty of conscience; and has given to the world the "Pilgrim's Progress" of Bunyan, such preachers as Robert Hall and Charles H. Spurgeon, and such missionaries as Carey and Judson.

"The Methodist Church, the Church of John Wesley, Charles Wesley and George Whitefield—three of the best and most apostolic Englishmen, abounding in useful labors, the first as a ruler and organizer, the second as a hymnist, the third as an evangelist—is a glorious church: for she produced the greatest religious revival since the day of Pentecost; she preaches a free and full salvation to all; she is never afraid to fight the devil, and she is hopefully and cheerfully marching on, in both hemispheres, as an army of conquest.

"The Society of Friends, though one of the smallest tribes in Israel, is a glorious society: for it has born witness to the inner light which 'lighteth every man that cometh into the world'; it has proved the superiority of the Spirit over all forms; it has done noble service in promoting tolerance and liberty, in prison reform, the emancipation of slaves, and other works of Christian philanthropy.

"The Brotherhood of the Moravians, founded by Count Zinzendorf—a true nobleman of nature and of grace—is a glorious brotherhood: for it is the pioneer of heathen missions and of Christian union among Protestant churches; it was like an oasis in the desert of German rationalism at home, while its missionaries went forth to the lowest savages in distant lands to bring them to Christ. I beheld with wonder and admiration a venerable Moravian couple devoting their lives to the care of hopeless lepers in the vicinity of Jerusalem.

"Nor should we forget the services of many who are accounted heretics.

"The Waldenses were witnesses of a pure and simple faith in times of superstition, and, having outlived many bloody persecutions, are now missionaries among the descendants of their persecutors.

"The Anabaptists and Socinians, who were so cruelly treated in the sixteenth century by Protestants and Romanists alike, were the first to aise their voice for religious liberty and the voluntary principle in religion.

"Unitarianism is a serious departure from the trinitarian faith of orthodox Christendom, but it did good service as a protest against tritheism, and against a stiff, narrow and uncharitable orthodoxy. It brought into prominence the human perfection of Christ's character, and illustrated the effect of His example in the noble lives and devotional writings of such men as Channing and Martineau. It has also given us some of our purest and sweetest poets, as Emerson, Bryant, Longfellow and Lowell, whom all good men must honor and love for their lofty moral tone.

"Universalism may be condemned as a doctrine; but it has a right to protest against a gross materialistic theory of hell with all its Dantesque horrors, and against the once widely-spread popular belief that the overwhelming majority of the human race, including countless millions of innocent infants, will forever perish. Nor should we forget that some of the greatest divines, from Origen and Gregory of Nyssa down to Bengel and Schleiermacher, believed in, or hoped for, the ultimate return of all rational creatures to the God of love, who created them in His own image and for His own glory.

"And, coming down to the latest organization of Christian work, which does not claim to be a church, but which is a help to all churches—the Salvation Army: we hail it, in spite of its strange and abnormal methods, as the most effective revival agency since the days of Wesley and Whitefield; for it descends to the lowest depths of degradation and misery, and brings the light and comfort of the Gospel to the slums of our large cities. Let us thank God for the noble men and women who, under the inspiration of the love of Christ, and unmindful of hardship, ridicule and persecution, sacrifice their lives to the rescue of the hopeless outcasts of society. Truly, these good Samaritans are an honor to the name of Christ and a benediction to a lost world."

The church of the future will be heir, conscious heir, with gratitude to God, to these priceless achievements, will gather them up as her own treasure, and one in Christ press forward to the conquest of the world.

APPENDIX.

"What are the Churches Going to Do About It?"

I beg leave to reprint as an appendix the following remarkable pamphlet which was issued by the eminently conservative gentlemen who sign it while I was preparing the manuscript for this book. T. D., Jr

Prefatory Note.

We pray your consideration of the facts herein presented. They have been gathered by the committee appointed at a meeting of pastors of various denominations, and were presented at a special meeting of clergymen and laymen representing several denominations.

At the latter meeting they were regarded of sufficient importance to become the basis of organization of the Federation of the Churches of New York City.

In preparing the circular letter accompanying this, it was found that there was need of presenting more fully the reasons why the churches should co-operate.

At the meeting on the twenty-first of October this statement was ordered to be printed and sent to each pastor in the city.

We therefore submit these facts, hoping that you will feel with us the desirability of such federation. Any doubt of the accuracy of the statistics herein presented emphasizes the need of securing a careful canvass of the whole city by interdenominational action.

In behalf of the Federation by the Special Committee,

   THE REV. ANSON P. ATTERBURY, D. D.
    " E. B. COE, D. D.
    " C. S. HARROWER, D. D.
    " J. M. PHILPUTT, D. D.
    " J. B. REMENSNYDER, D. D.
    " HENRY M. SANDERS, D. D.
    " HENRY A. STIMSON, D. D.
    " J. WINTHROP HEGEMAN, Ph. D.
            Chairman.

Relation of the Churches to Our Social Life.

The churches of New York City are not accomplishing their social mission. Any one may be convinced that this is a fact by a study of the average church life as related to the physical, economic, social and spiritual interests of the home life of our city.

Under the present condition of disunion, churchism and individualism, the churches never can accomplish their social mission.

Yet upon them rests the responsibility of securing the moral or spiritual foundation of social well-being, and of doing the constructive work of city civilization. The churches can do this. Only the churches can do it. By their aim they are committed to it. By their constitution they are fitted for it.

The 555 churches, with their clergy and 400,000 clientele, form first fruits of the new creation to be leaders and helpers of every home and social relations they come into touch with every human interest. By being organized into churches they have the capacity of direct action and possess various functions for the expression of their complete life.

Notwithstanding, there never has been put forth a serious and business-like effort to save New York City.

These members are the choice spirits of the city, owning more than one-fourth of our wealth, leaders in reforms, founders of charitable institutions and of colleges, and capable by concentrated effort, wisely directed, to effect any desirable purpose for social, civic or ecclesiastical well-being.

Instead of these resources having been used, it is the shameful truth that not one-hundreth part of the power of the churches is operative.

The aim of the churches is to bring all the interests of this line into harmony with the principles of the kingdom of heaven, to do the will of the Father on earth as it is done in heaven, and as first fruits of the new creation to be leaders of every movement movement working for righteousness.

The present arrangements for influencing society in accord with such a purpose would show that there has been no serious attempt made to realize that end. The average church life has fallen to the pitiable position of loyalty first to the church. It has even disclosed disloyalty to the Christ, in that its policies have not revealed that it has been loyal to the church for the sake of the Christ.

The churches know well that all social reforms begin among the humble citizens and work upward. Yet, in this most democratic country, the churches are our most aristocratic institutions, more aristocratic than those in any part of the world.

Church members voluntarily place themselves under the law of love to God and to neighbor as to self. This love works out ideal homes and a desire that other homes should be pure and clean and sweet. It is the source of public spirit when enlarged to the wish to secure best social conditions for all. It causes patriotism when extended to interests which work for national good.

Clergymen as a class have not shown love of neighboring clergymen as of selves. They have not expressed practical sympathy with the problems and conditions of the workingmen. They have not sought the salvation of those most needing it as conspicuously, at least, as those whose membership would enlarge their clientele. They have not been identified with movements to purify municipal life and to improve the conditions which make best American citizens.

The churches may disclaim the function of direct and corporate action, but they do affirm the theory of elevating society by diffusive personal influence.

Even in this position, the churches of New York City are not accomplishing their social mission.

Back of each church should be the whole church. The most meagre knowledge of our churches points to struggling churches, forlorn hopes, and pastors breaking down under the burden.

At the point of the strongest attack, reserves should be massed. There are no reserves, no central authority, no directing head.

Truth should be sown among the people. Up-town and central churches are elevators, shooting every week winnowed grain upon the same hearers. Not a grain for hundreds of thousands of citizens whose lives are worth cultivating and who starve for lack of the bread of life.

The lights are clustered and the dark places are blacker. The leaven and the masses are far apart. Not the ninety and nine are to be left and the one sought. To-day there are ninety astray and ten folded.

The leaven is placed as far away from business centres as convenient. The masses live as near to business as possible. Leavening is not an easy matter.

One who is thoroughly acquainted with the church and the charities it inspires may claim that there is no need or room for any more work. He may rightly point to organizations and functions for every imaginable need. He may catch the enthusiastic spirit of altruism everywhere abounding in good works. He may eloquently tell the story of the founding and results of our Department of Public Charities and Correction, public schools and night schools, Health Department, church charities, shelters, lodgings, nurseries, employment societies, asylums, hospitals, Charity Organization Society, Children's Aid, Improving the Condition of the Poor, and others equally commendable. He may affirm that such an exhibit is a better book on the evidences of Christianity than any ever written.

Yet, most of the misery met by these agencies could not exist had the churches done their duty in preventing the operation of causes producing these evils. The necessity of some of these institutions is a shame to our civilization.

We are not careful enough to destroy the germs of moral and social ills. Our zeal in trying to heal the disease is therefore less commendable.

If the churches cannot destroy the moral microbes and secure homes against a pestilential atmosphere by the inspiration of the Holy Spirit, they will surely fail in accomplishing their social mission.

In view of the emergency that confronts the churches, challenging their ability to meet it, in view of the heavy responsibilities weighting the churches to show that applied Christianity is adequate to elevate society to its ideal and normal condition, and considering the fact that the church has not yet made any earnest, concerted and scientific effort to act corporately or diffuse its resources adequately, the question is agitating—then, what are the churches going to do about it?

They will do nothing until they feel the necessity. They cannot do anything until they have data sufficient to see what should be done. We therefore submit evidences of existing conditions which make it impossible for the churches to fulfil their social mission in New York City. We point to a few of the causes which have produced these conditions.

Causes and Evidences.

The causes in the churches themselves which prevent the realization of the highest social mission are denominational individualism and "churchism." Denominational individualism has placed its churches without regard to interdenominational comity. Denominational glory has aroused the ambition of ministers. Churches have been located in reference to a good clientele, incidentally for saving all sorts and conditions of men.

Competition has been a principle of action. As a result we have to-day too many churches, and we have not enough churches. Too many for the church-goers. Too few for the real work to be done by churches. Too many in one locality. Too few where most needed.

Another effect has been overlapping of work, causing waste of workers and money. Between the interstices of this overlapping thousands of neglected souls have fallen to ruin.

Churchism determines the location of a church and its character by its clientele. It causes the church to exist for itself as an institution. As money must be had to support it, it must locate where a few wealthy people live, or where many well-to-do persons may be reached. As a result, the poor and those most needing saving influences are neglected.

The church on this basis must move with its supporting membership.

It has not heeded the law that if a church, as truly as a man, would save its life it must lose it. Consequently we have wealthy churches that are dead to the purpose of their real existence, and churches among the poor practically dead as to support and equipment, but behold, they live in the power of the spirit.

Also, churchism prevents a relization of the broader relations of the church to its denomination, to the church at large and to the kingdom. One cannot see the kingdom because of the churches.

By it church members cannot have the inspiration of the highest motives which cause liberality, personal service and spirituality.

These causes have prevented any interdenominational effort to swing the resources of the churches against evils which threaten social well-being, and any comity which might secure such a distribution of churches as to man every strategic position with strongest Christian influences.

We place in evidence the situation of the churches, showing how inadequately denominationalism and churchism have caused the location of centres of Christian work.

The canvass of St. Augustine's parish under the auspices of the Church Temperance Society has given valuable statistics which we may use in connection with our own study of church distribution in the city.

One district with a population of 16,391 bodies has one saloon to every 111 inhabitants, and one church to every 8,196. (See chart No. 1.)

This means that it pays brewers to locate saloons among the poorest classes. It means that the church members possessing one-fourth of our wealth evidently do not think that it will pay to put there more than one church to over 8,000 souls. Each of these churches has at least 7,000 persons outside of its clientele whom it cannot possibly reach by even its indirect influences. What are the churches going to do about it?

The situation is worse in another district, with one saloon to every 158, and one church to every 9,422. (See charts No. 2.)

The saloon has been to hundreds the only shelter on wild, stormy nights. The churches are occasionally open to satisfy a desire which is felt by only a few. The churches are never crowded beyond their capacity, which is adequate for the demand.

It should be noted that with decreasing church privileges comes shrinkage of church clientage. With increasing of church staff of workers comes improvement of neighborhood and faith in the church. Beyond the reach of these churches are 8,000 souls for each church. What are the churches going to do about it?

In the third district the situation is worst of all. Among 49,359 inhabitants there is one saloon to every 208, one church to every 9,872. With such a ratio what are the churches going to do to save our city? Such evidence that these people do not want the church is the very reason why the churches should distribute their full energy among them so as to cause them to want a church. (See charts No. 3.)

It has been estimated that the 90,000 inhabitants of this parish pay annually into the saloons an average per individual of $75. The average amount paid by each church member every year to all church expenses and work is not over $30. It may readily be seen that if these people want a church they can pay for it. To make them want it—that's the crux of all our work. The sadness of it is that they care less and less for it, because they feel that no one cares for them. Were the whole energy of the churches put forth at once, it would be too late to bring this generation into the Kingdom. It is not too late to save the children.

In this one parish 27,000 souls beyond the touch of the churches! What are the churches going to do about it?

We submit the condition of churches as related to social life below 14th Street. With a population of about 700,000 what can the few churches do toward the constructive work of our civilization? From January to May of this year six of our most active pastors have resigned because they could not endure the strain and because the resources at their command were pitiably inadequate to relieve the distress which begged assistance.

Including in church clientage all children and occasional attendants, there are, outside of the direct touch of church influences, about 400,000 souls.

What can the 8 Baptist churches with 2,992 members effect alone there? Or the efficient city missions with 2,500 members?

Or both combined with 7 Reformed churches, 6 Lutheran, 16 Presbyterian, 18 Methodist, 21 Jewish, 22 Episcopal and 28 Roman Catholic? One hundred and thirty-five churches, including small missions and schools, are doing all that they can with the means at their command. Add to them the charitable institutions and residential settlements and distribute all agencies so that in each ward every social need should be met by a special function for its relief, still the churches would be powerless to perform their function of transforming home-life by personal regeneration. Outward changes of circumstances without inner change of life is labor in perpetuity.

We have made special investigations of a section on the west side of the city up-town. This section includes the old Ninth, Thirteenth, Fifteenth and Seventeenth Assembly Districts, containing about 200,000 inhabitants. The churches distributed there are 7 Baptist, 1 Lutheran, 9 Methodist, 6 Presbyterian, 5 Reformed and United Presbyterian, 7 Episcopal, 12 Roman Catholic, and 9 other denominations. (See charts No. 5.)

Every church or chapel is worked to its utmost, and yet there are more than 100,000 souls beyond the reach of all these churches.

In a section between 24th and 59th Streets, west of Eighth Avenue, there is but one church to 10,561 of population.

In the same, west of Ninth Avenue, one church to 14,580; west of Tenth Avenue, one to 31,926.

West of Tenth Avenue, between 40th and 64th Streets, there is only one church. There are 46,563 people living in that district.

It must not be thought that there are not enough churches within reach of these multitudes if they wished to go to them. The significance lies in the fact that the churches are not doing anything to cause them to wish to go. Also, that such people are not desirable material for membership of church life as based on "Churchism." They are not material for the clientele of the churches. Therefore they are not sought and churches are not placed in their midst.

It is said that between 86th and 138th Streets, east of Fifth Avenue, there are 223,000 souls, and that a certain denomination has but one church in that district. In the same district, west of Fifth Avenue, there are 72,000 souls, and this denomination has nine churches among them. This illustrates "churchism! (See chart No. 5.)

When throughout the city you trace the direct and indirect influences of church life upon the people you find a churchless population as large as the city of Brooklyn.

What are the churches going to do about it?

The full significance of these statistics is not felt until an analysis is made of the intellectual, social, civic, economic and spiritual condition of the churchless masses.

Each individual is a person. Personality is the greatest thing in the universe.

Some of these churchless ones are homeless. Thousands live in cheap boarding houses; 360,000 in the slums. According to Carroll Wright's census, 37.69 per cent. are unable to read or write, 52.44 per cent. are voters, 62.38 per cent. were born in countries in a civilization foreign to the genius of our institutions. In our tenements there is an average of 37 persons to a dwelling.

The unit of the social organism is the home. The type of larger social life is found in the relationships of family life.

The specific object of social work by the churches should be the child. In these tenements are 147,000 children under five years of age; 50,000 are school truants. Thousands are compelled to work who should be at school or at play.

Bad homes make bad children. Over half of the young criminals in Elmira Penitentiary come from bad homes.

Bad streets make them worst; 97 per cent. in this penitentiary come from bad street associates.

Bad surroundings destroy possibility of mature strength. The diseases of 600 children examined were traced to their surroundings and not to hereditary predisposition. Medical examination of 530 of the tenement children showed that only 60 were healthy.

Ignorance of how to live and how to meet emergencies causes loss of life. "Poverty and ignorance kill and cripple more than disease germs."

The children of parents who, when very young, were made to work are predestinated to criminal careers, idiocy, imbecility or insanity.

"Child labor, the source of untold miseries to society, has increased during the last fifteen years over 100 per cent. This, in spite of compulsory laws." In 1887 the Commissioner of Labor for New York State officially wrote: "Year by year we have seen an increase in the demand for smaller and smaller children until it became a veritable robbery of the cradle to supply them."

Ex-Supt. Byrnes has said: "The tenement is one of the biggest cogs in the machine that makes criminals. Its associations are dangerous to the purity of women and the honesty of men. It is certain that the overcrowding of tenements must fill children's minds with vicious and wicked knowledge."

What are the churches going to do about it?

The church at large has not lifted its voice against these evil conditions or swung its forces as a unit in behalf of the social, civic, industrial or spiritual elevation of these homes.

It is moral character that affects our social and civic conditions and largely fixes economic values.

We submit that character-making is a function of the churches. This will always be left to the churches. In view of the evidences what are they going to do about it?

Federation of the Churches—The Remedy.

The problem for the churches to solve is how to bring such conditions into harmony with the laws and ideals of the Kingdom of God.

Before anything can be done, social facts must be carefully ascertained so that we may know what is needed. The work of existing societies must be examined so that its value may be determined, its lack supplemented and its weakness made strong. The resources and reserves of the churches must be applied to overthrow evils and to maintain whatever is good. Loyalty to the Christ must precede loyalty to the church. The true aim of the body of Christ must clearly be kept in sight. The harmonious working of its members must be secured.

The method of Christ and of the Apostles in working reform from the bottom of society upward must be adopted by the churches. The Church of Jesus Christ is eminently for workingmen. The "Labor Church" can never be a substitute for it. Human well-being must be sought directly for the sake of the man, without any reference to even indirect gain to the church.

The present arrangements and locations of churches and agencies need readjusting to secure economy and greatest efficiency. The power of the whole church must be felt to be behind each church in order that the weakest may be honored—just as the whole personality is back of the function of each member of our body.

It must be maintained that the churches are adequate to effect social reforms. That the passionate altruism which is doing so much in organizing relief for every possible need cannot take the place of the personal sympathy and love inspired by the Christ as a transforming or reforming agent. That socialism of city or State simply throws upon the churches a heavier degree of responsibility to form the best character.

We must remember that after twenty years of "Practicable Socialism" in East London, Canon Barnett, of Toynbee, confesses to disappointment in the results—"the standard of life is still far lower than it should be."

It is evident that such a problem appeals to all the churches. No one denomination can work it out. Each denomination is inextricably involved in it. The solution demands interdenominational action—not undenominational. United effort of all churches is necessary whenever public sentiment is to be agitated or public opinion directed in right direction.

Instead of united sentiment and clearness of testimony, we have had an occasional sermon, a casual recommendation, an official deliverance. Nothing concentrated—no action all along the line.

To cause the opinion of the churches to be respected, there should be a common expression through some common medium. To direct opinion, the church and press should unite in simultaneous agitation on all social and civic interests.

Interdenominational action is necessary to secure means to prevent waste by overlapping of work, to voice common sentiment, express common sympathy, apply the concentrated power of the churches when necessary, to co-ordinate the work of the charitable institutions, to use their functions and strengthen their effectiveness, and to do everything to realize the social mission of the kingdom of Christ.

It seems that the most practicable method by which interdenominational action may effect such an end is federation of the individual churches. Such federation would secure a representative body which, through its members, would practically unite all the churches on a common basis and be in touch with each of them.

It would elect a Central Council, made up of one clergyman and one lay member from each denomination. This Council, while having no authority over the co-operating churches, would be the governing body of the Federation. It would appoint commissions and committees, and recommend such action to the consideration of the co-operating churches as would tend to secure the social mission of the churches.

The discussion of its recommendations and the presentation of the ascertained needs of our city by experts would practically form an interdenominational social union with its many advantages.

It would furnish an occasion for the interchange of methods of church work and the discussion of questions of mutual interest.

It would present to the world an object lesson of the structure of the kingdom—each denomination preserving its individuality and all co-operating in love and strength for the purpose of bringing the joy of heaven into the homes on earth.

It would show the practical creed of all the denominations.

It would affirm the living Christ as the basis of union.

It would present a sense of united action from which would arise a motive so strong that under its pressure workers and money would be consecrated to the work of saving the homes of our city.

It would awaken a power which intelligently directed and persistently applied could effect any desired reform.

This, we believe, is the only practicable remedy under present conditions. The time is ripe for it. The pressing question then is, "What is my church going to do about it? Canton Westcott has said: "If the church is to perform its social function there must not be a single person in it without a ministry for others. The way of action will be made clear as soon as the spirit of action has gained power."

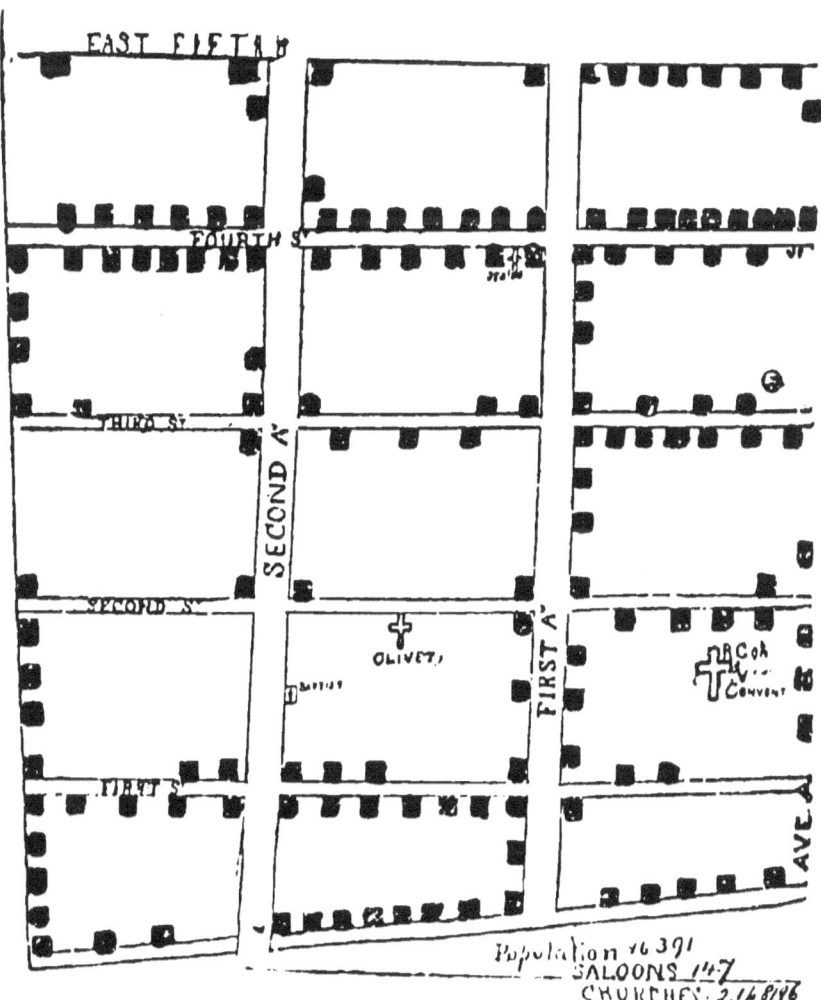

CHART No. 1.

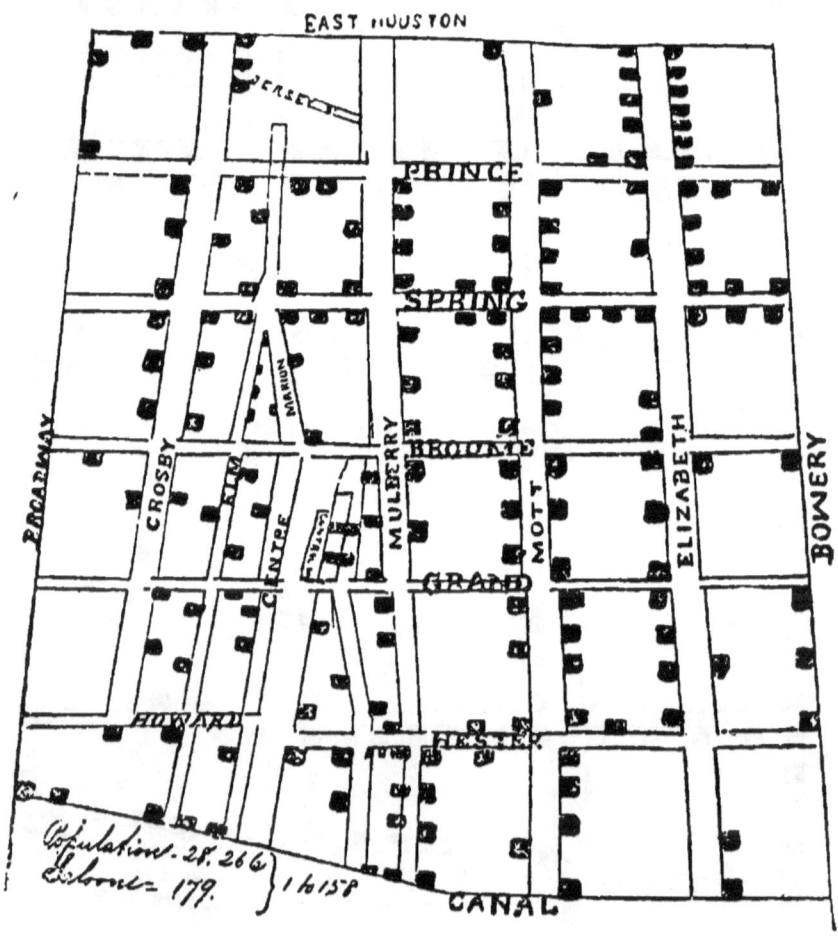

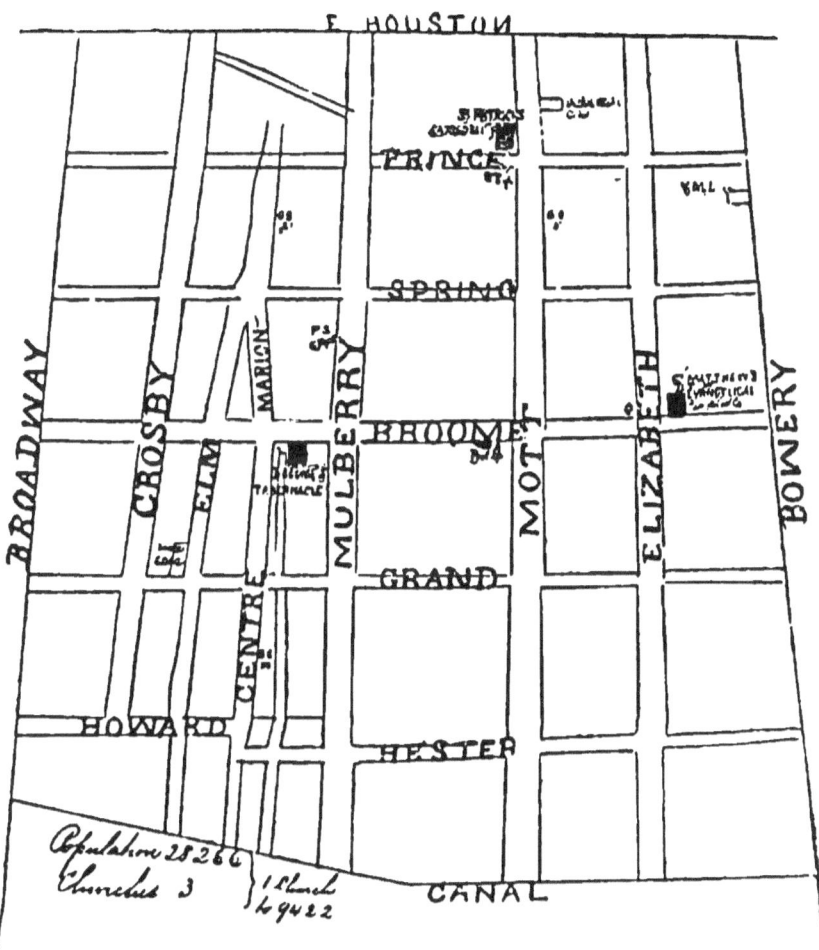

No. 2.

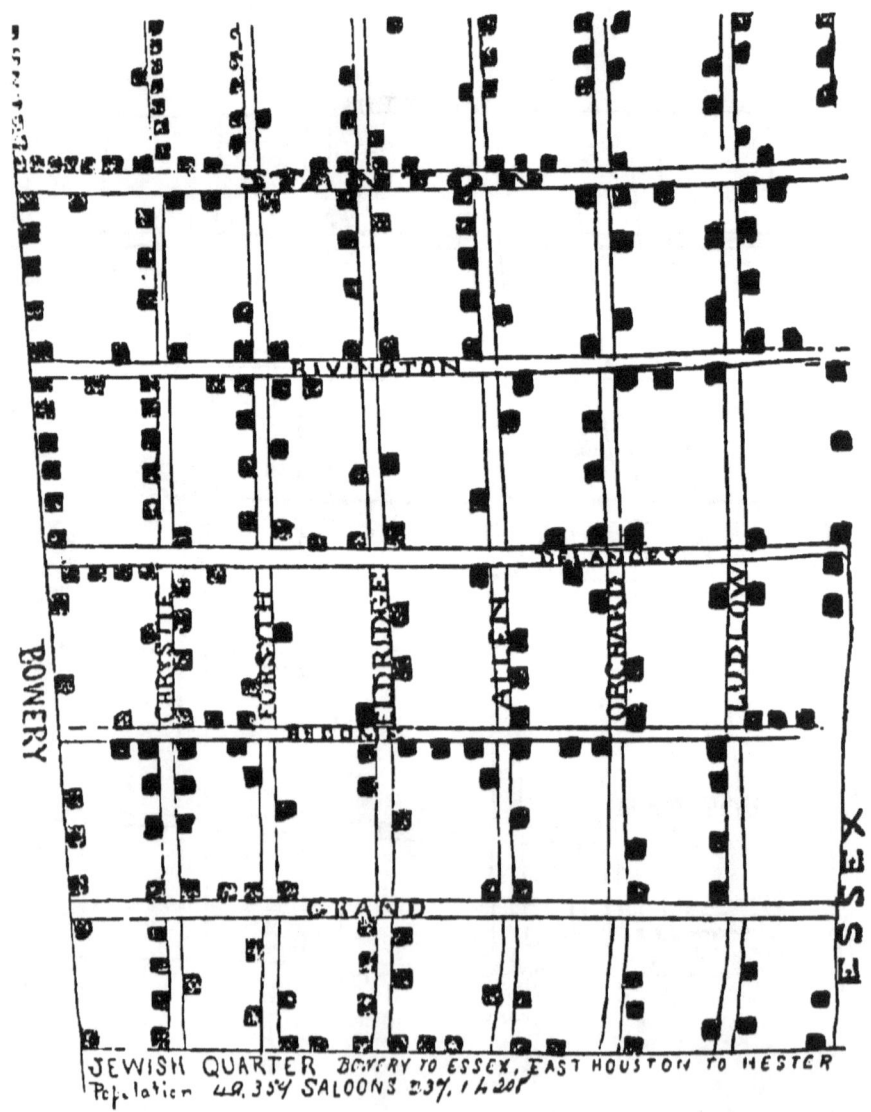

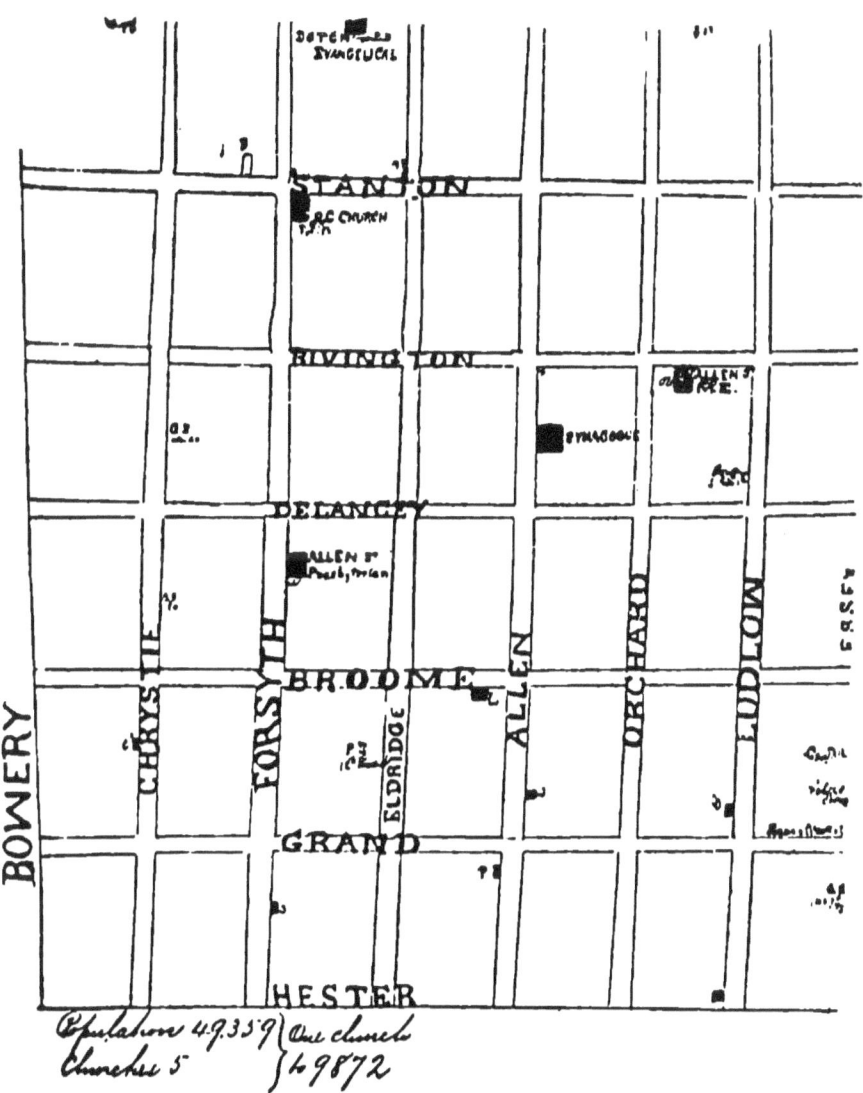

No. 3.

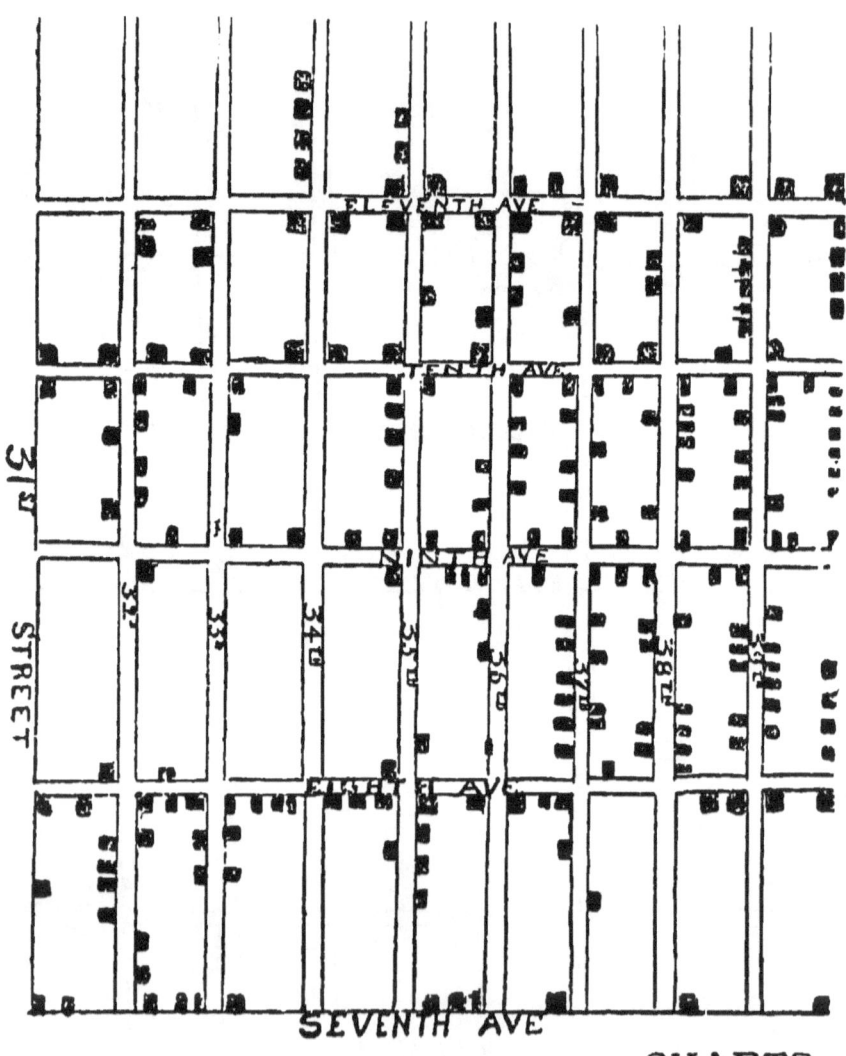

CHARTS

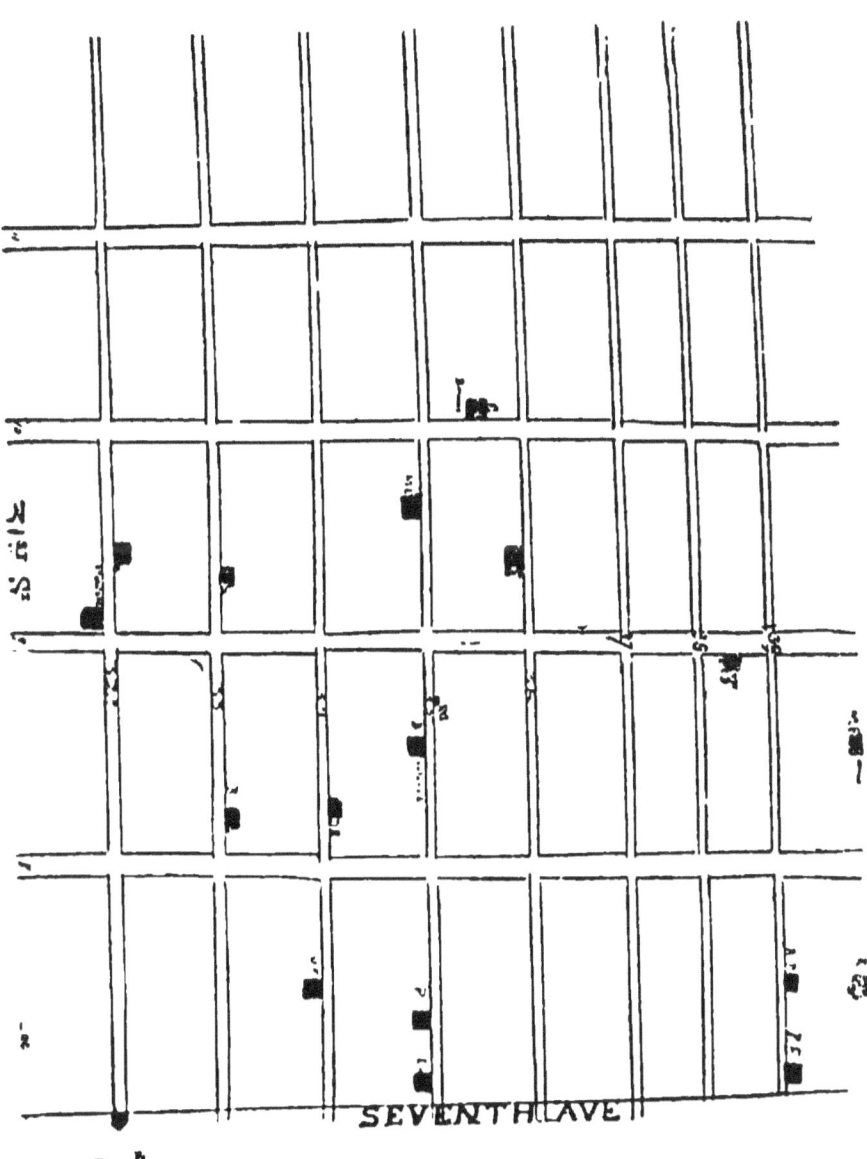

www.ingramcontent.com/pod-product-compliance
Lightning Source LLC
Chambersburg PA
CBHW030334170426
43202CB00010B/1126